T0113825

Oman

Stories from a Modern Arab Country

Stig Pors Nielsen

authorHOUSE®

AuthorHouse™ UK Ltd.
1663 Liberty Drive
Bloomington, IN 47403 USA
www.authorhouse.co.uk
Phone: 0800.197.4150

© 2014 Stig Pors Nielsen. All rights reserved.

No part of this book may be reproduced, stored in a retrieval system, or
transmitted by any means without the written permission of the author.

Published by AuthorHouse 07/28/2014

ISBN: 978-1-4969-8771-6 (sc)
ISBN: 978-1-4969-8770-9 (hc)
ISBN: 978-1-4969-8772-3 (e)

Any people depicted in stock imagery provided by Thinkstock are models,
and such images are being used for illustrative purposes only.
Certain stock imagery © Thinkstock.

This book is printed on acid-free paper.

Because of the dynamic nature of the Internet, any web addresses or links contained in
this book may have changed since publication and may no longer be valid. The views
expressed in this work are solely those of the author and do not necessarily reflect the
views of the publisher, and the publisher hereby disclaims any responsibility for them.

Contents

Prologue

Oman occupies the south-eastern corner of the Arab peninsula. The country is beautiful, full of unspoiled nature. The sun shines almost every day. The temperature is agreeable during the winter months, but it is often unbearably hot during summer. The country is as large as Italy, but in 1994, there were only around one million Omanis, and a little more than half a million expatriates.

The Omani population is growing rapidly. The country has many natural resources in the form of oil, gas, and minerals. It is blessed with a ruler, His Majesty Sultan Qaboos, who has what one might call total power, which he uses with great wisdom. He is the servant of his people.

When I came to this country, he had ruled for twenty-four years. Now, at my latest visit, forty-four years have passed since His Majesty took over in 1970. My short stories were written in 1995 and during later visits because I wanted to remember this beautiful country with its charming population, which in fewer than fifty years has achieved what Europe needed five hundred years to accomplish.

May others be interested.

Acknowledgements

I thank my friends Mrs Ruth Rollitt and Mr Philip Rollitt for their time-consuming language revisions. I also want to thank all the Omanis and Westerners I have met in Oman. They have inspired me to write this book.

In particular I want to thank

Hospital Director Nasser Lamki, MD

Professor Sven-EricLindell, MD, Med. Dr.

Professor Nicholas Woodhouse, MD

Senior Consultant Haddia Bererhi, MD

Head of Khoula Hospital Wahid Al Kharusi, MD

Professor Bengt Linder, MD

Stig Pors Nielsen

Copenhagen and Muscat, 2014

Chapter 1

In which one arrives, acquires telephone, goes on an excursion, and celebrates Christmas, the ascension of the prophet, and our New Year

Arrival

Arriving at the international airport of Muscat in August 1994, un-acclimatized as we were, we most of all wanted to strip off our clothes and skin in order to sit in the shade in our bare skeletons. It was unbearably hot and humid. Later we were told the temperature was fifty-five degrees Celsius.

I had accepted an offer to come to Muscat and work for a year as a senior consultant at the university hospital, temporarily leaving my job in Denmark. The time of arrival was carefully chosen because the academic year starts at the beginning of September, and I was supposed to be teaching medical students as well as doing diagnostic work at the department of clinical physiology, the only one of its kind in the Middle East. Everything was, as expected, difficult. A change of environment becomes more difficult with age, and I was fifty-eight. The Omanis were, however, extremely nice and helpful all the time. Colleagues and co-workers did their best to make us feel at home, and we did. The first problem, though, was communication with the outside world.

Telephone

We had decided television was not necessary and that we could live without a telephone. Television is, as is well-known, not good for the creativity, and we managed without this new invention, which changes people in an unwanted direction (in our opinion). It turned out, however, that it was more difficult to live without a telephone. We wanted to be able to contact family, friends, and colleagues at home. Therefore, after a few weeks, we decided we would acquire a telephone. It turned out there was a long way from making this decision to actually having a phone.

Firstly, the university told me I had to pay a deposit of three hundred Omani rials, corresponding to five thousand Danish kroner (DKK), not a small amount for a man with a moderate income. I thought they could have told me beforehand. Naturally the deposit was introduced because a person had left the country without paying his bill. I now had to produce a copy of my contract and my passport and photos, all to be delivered at the university, which then could prove to the telephone company that I actually was the person I claimed to be. (They of course already had all papers, but that is another matter.)

In this country, there are many office clerks wanting to demonstrate their importance. Here was one. He said there should be a copy of the contract in Arabic, presumably because he could not read English. Incidentally, they already had a copy in Arabic. However, I had to produce one, and I did. Hereafter I could drive to the telephone company, a building in the centre of Muscat, far away. I told my department that I would be away for a couple of hours. It turned out not to be true.

The domicile of the telephone company of Oman (Omantel) was a big building with numerous employees. A buzz of activity sounded. I quickly realized this was not synonymous with efficiency. I approached one of the desks, gave my papers to somebody, and was asked to wait. I did. There was time to watch the surroundings. Some had come to pay their telephone bill, which was understandable, although it seems there might be other ways to pay than turning up at the phone company. Paying your bill here seemed to be rather complicated. It took time. Only one of the thirty-five employees was dealing with this important problem. The rest were reading the newspaper or looking out the window.

At a conspicuous spot sat an elderly Omani gentleman. He was picking his nose and other natural orifices of his head while he studied the newspaper with interest. Judging from his speed of reading, he could not read. After an hour he left, apparently for lunch.

Another Omani took his place. He also started picking his nose and reading the newspaper. No costumers asked the two gentlemen for help, so what they actually were expected to do remained a secret.

My European impatience took over. I approached one of the desks. No, there was nothing new. I asked for the boss and learned he was called Abdullah. After some time I found Abdullah in another room. He was apparently a very important man. That was easy to see, because he had two telephones, a red one and a white one. He spoke into both simultaneously, something he probably had seen on film. In this country, where phones are rather new, it must be a sign of high status to possess two of them. Another sign of high status was the fact that he had six secretaries. Apparently none of them worked. Each had a telephone which, however, none of them used. And I had none.

Abdullah continued to talk into both phones. I sat humbly in a chair into which I was asked to place my body, and studied the secretaries. One showed me with pride a wedding gift she was in the process of producing for her sister. It was nice: a sort of a bush with money notes attached to its branches. Another one talked to a colleague. I did not understand a word. My Arabic is rather poor. It must have been very funny, because they laughed all the time. The last three ladies sat staring at nothing, apparently waiting for somebody to call them. Nobody did. Abdullah was still talking after one hour. I coughed discretely.

Well, was there were anything he, Abdullah, could do for me? he asked very friendly.

"Well, yes. I would appreciate your help acquiring a telephone apparatus," I told him in English, which he understood and spoke well. Had I brought four hundred rials? "No, I have only three hundred rials," I said with despair, adding that my friend, the hospital director, had said three hundred rials, not four hundred. Well, that was correct because I was a doctor. So far, so good. I then asked the man if he would need the money right away.

"Oh, no." The idea was appalling. The amount should be paid at the telephone ministry. But first I should be given a telephone number. That was easy to understand. Without a telephone number, no telephone. Abdullah asked me if I would kindly re-enter the hall where I came from. I did.

A little later, Abdullah entered the hall. He gave the job of the day to one of the idle clerks. That job was supposed to be done in half an hour, I was told. A telephone number. That cannot be difficult. After some time the clerk had found out there was no telephone number available. I was upset, but that did not help, Abdullah would call my department. When I came back, exhausted, Abdullah had called just before closing time, confirming there was no available telephone number.

The next day I went to see my friend, the hospital director, Nasser. I explained to him that I was the only doctor at the university hospital, who did not have a telephone.

That did not disturb him. "But," he said," I will do you a favour." He would call the top boss at the telephone company of Oman, asking if I would be given one of the six telephone lines available for His Majesty Sultan Qaboos. (He has those in case he one day would be a patient here, at his own hospital.) He has himself paid the hospital with his private money.

I felt honoured, thanked Nasser, and left his office. The next day there was a message for me, asking me to contact the famous man who had the authority to give me one of His Majesty's telephone lines. That man was very efficient. He had only one telephone, but it could do anything. He also had a PC, and he could use it. His English was fluent. Everything was fixed in five minutes. I paid before I left.

Now only two problems remained: How to get a telephone apparatus and get it installed. This would not be simple. I was asked to find a newly built house in Al Hail, which rather practically is situated forty-five kilometres from the other telephone offices. There are no numbers on the houses here, but I thought I could find it from the description given to me.

After some hours I did find it. There were six Omanis wearing typical Omani dress, not allowed for foreigners, and an Indian man wearing a turban. Modest as I now was, I addressed one of the Omanis. He did not understand me well (not all Omanis have a good command of English), so to be sure he mumbled that it was impossible. I now asked the Indian, who it turned out spoke English and Arabic fluently. He then explained my problem in Arabic to the Omanis. Leaving the office with the final piece of paper, I got assurances that the telephone would come tomorrow. I chose to believe it.

Before leaving I thanked the Indian, saying it was obvious one should always go to the boss directly.

"Oh, no," he said. He was not the boss, he was the cleaner.

The telephone came the next day. Now the Western world was no longer isolated from us.

Wadi Bashing

We were "bashing" in the *wadis* (the riverbeds), which are normally dry, in our car. (Wadi bashing is about riding through wadis in a four-wheeler.) If one wants to see Oman, one needs an "off-roader," a four-wheel-drive car of the solid type. I had the same model as His Majesty: a Land Rover Discovery. If that model was good enough for the Sultan, it is good enough for me. His was a bit more refined than mine, in that his had two water bags hanging from the front, symbolizing his carriage was kind of a camel. It had eight cylinders, ten forward gears, and a "differential lock," to be used in soft sand, ensuring you were not easily stuck, all wheels turning at the same speed. This particular car was a bit thirsty, but petrol was inexpensive here. You were sitting high, like in a Ford from the twenties. That high position makes driving safer in case of collision. There are many traffic accidents here, where traffic rules exist but are often forgotten. They are regarded as guidelines by some Omanis.

It is a golden rule here that you do not move away from known paths or roads into a wadi without being accompanied by at least one other car. Your car can break down, and then it is not easy to return home. This country is beautiful, also seen from motorways, but nothing is comparable to the beauty of the wadis. Often one drives on the stony bottom of the wadi, sometimes on gravel roads in the mountains with a breathtaking view that makes it tempting to stop, but that can be dangerous in case of a forty-five-degree slope. Like in the desert, it is important to keep moving. You have to drive extremely carefully. You are not protected and you can fall down, killing yourself and your passengers.

Driving on the bottom of a wadi is often exciting, but not without potential danger. It has happened that people have drowned in their cars even though the wadi was dry at the beginning of their tour. What you can expose yourself to is a flash flood: It has been raining in the mountains, perhaps a hundred kilometres away from where you are. There might not be a cloud in the sky, but suddenly a big wave comes, like a wall of water, several meters high. Some months ago a number of young men and girls departed to have a swim in a wadi pool, where the water is often cool. It can be tempting to bathe in a cool wadi pool, especially in the hot season. We are, however, never tempted, since we know there can be malaria here. Particularly dangerous is the time of sunset, the blue hour, where the mosquitoes are particularly active. The young people had their swim. Without warning a flash flood came which killed six out of the eight youngsters.

One of my colleagues at the university hospital was driving at the bottom of a wadi, where he parked his car. He and his family were walking on the edges of the wadi.

His nine-year old daughter said, "Dad, listen. There is an odd sound. What is it?"

The father knew. He hastily ran downwards, into his car, switched on the engine, drove upwards from where he with his family watched a flash flood passing by. My colleague does not park at the bottom of a wadi anymore. One should perhaps not drive in wadis, but we believe in our ability to get away when needed.

Once we passed a narrow part of a wadi, there was a vertical measuring device like a giant ruler with a scale from zero to five meters. It had been in use recently. When a flash flood has passed, there remains small ponds of water with small fish and frogs. Unfortunately, these spots of animal life are now disappearing, since underground draining tubes are now being installed to save water, which is a precious commodity in this part of the world.

The fact that human beings can actually live in the barren country of the wadis may seem odd. They survive due to the water from the mountains. Over centuries, people have built and maintained terraces and canals for irrigation of the fields on the terraces. That was an art taught by the Persians who in olden times occupied the country. An irrigation canal is termed a *falaj*. It can mean survival for the people in the mountain villages. These *aflāj* (plural of falaj) are maintained by the men in common. At the upper part of a falaj, one may drink the water. Farther down one may wash one's body and clothes, and finally the water is used for irrigation. There are strict rules for the usage of the water. Water pollution is strictly forbidden. Alone you can do nothing, but in conjunction with other men you can do a lot. Sometimes the men have to dig deep down to get the water under a hill. So they do. Impressive art of engineering. We have in the village Rustaq falaj being utilized for public baths.

We often discuss why Westerners like the wadis so much. I think it has something to do with the barren landscape with a variety of impressive colours. Geologists love the wadis. Nowhere else in the world can one study geology without disturbing greenery. At certain places you can study the entire history of our planet. You start at one end of a wadi where the rocks are sixteen million years old, coming to even older structures, ending by standing on rocks which are six hundred million years old.

Natural Resources and Geology

Our geologists at the university have a lot to do. Twenty-five years ago this country was practically unknown to geologists. Oil and gas have been found, and there is more to be discovered. PDO is the country's biggest company. (PDO stands for Petroleum Development of Oman.) PDO employs a substantial number of geologists. In order to please His Majesty, PDO some years ago produced a book on the geology of Oman, filled with wonderful pictures and interesting text. I have had it in my hands. Unfortunately it cannot be bought. Competitors might get ideas of drilling or mining.

Celebrating the twenty-fifth anniversary of the Renaissance (1970, the year when Sultan Qaboos took over), one of the geologists from the university published a field guide to the geology of northern Oman, the northern tip Musandam included. This peninsula, which looks like Norway with fjords and cliffs, is isolated from the rest of Oman, surrounded as it is by UAE (United Arab Emirates). Why does it belong to Oman? Because the sheiks in this part of the country long ago voted they wanted to be ruled by the ruler of Oman, not by the emirs farther north. So it is an exclave. Musandam is internationally important because the tip of Musandam is adjacent to the Straits of Hormuz. The country which possesses Musandam can stop any traffic in those vital waterways through which passes a significant part of the oil consumed by the Western world. No surprise that His Majesty is courted by the important world powers, Iran included, a country with which Oman has always had good relations. It is said that some years ago the United States, without avail, tried to press the Sultan to cool down the warm relations with Iran. His Majesty might be a friend of the United States, but he knows best what is good for Oman. He refused. With the aid of the novel field guide, one can be guided through the northern part of Oman, so we can not only enjoy the landscape, but also be able to understand why everything in northern Oman is so breathtakingly beautiful.

Numerous metals have been found in the mountains of Oman (e.g., gold, silver, and chromium, not forgetting copper, which was exported to Mesopotamia thousands of years ago). The old copper mines were the basis for the bronze age in Mesopotamia and later Europe. Copper was mined in enormous quantities. The old mines are now being excavated by archaeologists.

One does not often think of the fact that life on Earth is a rather new phenomenon, and that man arrived here a few minutes before midnight New Year's Eve, if the history of our globe is like a year of 365 days.

Let us start with the beginning: our planet is 3800 million years old. Every day of our theoretical calendar year is around 10 million years. Thus measuring, it must be stated that very little is known from January to July. Primitive life begins in July or August; crustaceans start to appear in November. Dinosaurs arrive 10 December and disappear 25 December, thus being here 15 days corresponding to 125 million years. We humans are beginners on this planet.

The oldest proofs of life on Earth are found here in the wadis: fossilized primitive algae, the so-called stromatolites, which are around six hundred million years old. We have seen them ourselves. They live on some places on Earth but also in our local waters, it is said. Bacteria might have come earlier but left no traces. Overall in Oman, fossils of maritime animals are found (e.g., snails and mussels, but others are also found, some of which have been extinct for millions of years). Even in the mountains at three thousand meters altitude fossilized sea animals can be found. I have a big snail fossil said to be ninety million years old. Originally it lived on the bottom of a seabed long gone. I got it from a lady who lives here at three thousand meters altitude.

To the left of the main road to the university is a gravel plain. Here is the greatest chance to find fossilized dinosaur remnants. Many have been found here, often in conglomerates, five hundred meters from where I am writing this. The finds are exhibited at university. I have not yet found anything, but I am still looking. A fossil dinosaur egg would be nice to find. Such eggs can be converted to cash, well paid as they are at auctions in London. When one goes dinosaur hunting, one should be careful, using boots and gloves, as scorpions hide comfortably below stones.

Oman has tried everything during the last eight hundred million years. For a long period, present Oman was seabed, but there are also stripes in rocks suggesting a distant ice age. During two periods, the country which is today Oman was situated not far from the South Pole. There are traces of volcanic activities overall, lava having hardened during underwater cooling. There are mountains with rocky material pushed over layers of former seabed, sediments in irregular, often very beautiful forms, witnesses of the strong forces of nature.

People and Animals in the Wadis

Back to present times: snakes are rather common in the wadis, especially near non-moving water, where they feed on frogs. It is a good idea to throw a stone into the water if you intend to bathe in a wadi pool. However, we do not often think of snakes, nor do we fear them. Perhaps we should.

One day during a wadi trip, I wanted to take a photo of my superintendent, David. A giant rock, twenty meters tall, ten meters thick, but only a couple of meters at the base looked as it could fall over. David standing on the stone would be a worthy motive. He climbed this odd stone which had probably had its present position for millions of years. He hurried back before he had reached his final position. Why? Did he not like it up there? Yes, but a one meter-long snake had appeared. It looked scary. We consulted our snake book which we incidentally had with us. It was one of the foul ones, and we were far away from a hospital with anti-venom. However, although frightening, the snakes here are not as dangerous as the snakes of Australia or those living in the sea here in Oman. I shall come back to those later.

There are not many people here, only as many as the wadis can feed. There were more in earlier days it seemed, as judged from the number of terraces no longer being cultivated. A couple of thousand years earlier the inhabitants of Wadi Bani Karusi had made impressive drawings on the rock walls, depicting people and animals which are now extinct in Oman (e.g., giraffes). My colleague Wahid al Karusi comes from this wadi. He is the chief orthopaedic surgeon of His Majesty. I know him well. He belongs to Omani nobility. He invited me to lecture at his hospital on osteoporosis. It went well. Once we met him at the airport at three o'clock in the morning, a time of activity due to late arriving and departing aircraft. He was waiting for somebody. His status was of a kind that helped us through customs in no time. He laughs easily.

As said, there are few people living in the wadis. And there are not so many wild animals as in earlier days, but we have wolves and leopards, and some giant lizards, often seventy-five centimetres long. Their meat is said to be delicious, almost like chicken. Women scream when they see them. Unfortunately, we no longer have lions, but it is well known from antiquity that lions used to be common in this part of the world. There is a variety of antelopes, like the oryx, a beautiful large and greyish animal with black markings and long horns, which disappeared from the deserts of Southern Arabia, Oman included. They were shot and eaten. His Majesty who thinks of everything, decided a few of those precious animals should be bought from European zoological gardens, where there were some survivors. The purchased animals started to breed under supervision. Now there are plenty. It is strictly forbidden to shoot them.

Some students at the university were told about this undertaking. One said cleverly, "Then we can chase them across the border into Saudi Arabia and shoot them there." Well, well.

There are numerous small and large caves in the Hajar Mountains with access from the adjacent wadis, but so far we have not heard of earlier human habitation there. The caves are not extensively explored, though. Recently a visiting Austrian team of cave explores came to investigate one of the world's most extensive cave systems which is located here. We have not yet heard of their results, so we do not know if there were traces of earlier human activity, like in France and Spain.

The present inhabitants of the wadis live in small villages where there is water. We have seen villages which have been abandoned due to lack of water, old falaj no longer in use, and some graves of the type beehive graves, remnants from times long gone. In olden times graves were more elaborate than today (e.g., in the village of Bat, where Danish archaeologists have recently been digging).

People living in the wadis are traditionally dressed. The women wear colourful long dresses, and long trousers with silver embroidery, often with silver jewellery, popular among women from Europe and the United States. The men seldom move around without their rifles. They do not smile a lot, and look somewhat frightening. We do our best not to offend them with our Western clothing and behaviour.

Recently we spotted two young American girls sunbathing in their bikinis on a rock in a wadi. An Omani man with his rifle saw them. He did not shoot them, but judging from his face he did not like what he saw. I thought they looked quite beautiful. It should, however, be remembered that Omanis do not like Westerners to expose themselves as did the two girls. The Omani men and women are extremely shy and very private. That should be respected by visitors.

Christmas

It was pleasantly warm, not hot. Any idea of eating indoor was abandoned. It was not that warm. So we celebrated Christmas on the terrace. A Christmas tree had been purchased for the purpose; it was planted in one of our spacious pots. The skies were clear, and the stars were sparkling. The moon was beaming down, and everything was like in Bethlehem two thousand years ago. No snow, no Father Christmas. We danced round the Christmas tree, singing Danish Christmas hymns and carols. We listened out for possible reactions from our Muslim neighbours. They said nothing.

One is tolerant here. In Saudi Arabia we could not have done it. We would have been arrested, jailed, or with luck quickly deported. And in Saudi Arabia we could not have been consuming alcohol.

Danish ducks were purchased at the local supermarket. We had some problems finding the right spices, but everything went well. Since we were so far way from our native country, it was rather easy to de-commercialize Christmas.

All the family members were assembled. They had come to pay us a visit, so we were seven in the house. That was no problem. The houses at the university campus were made for big families. It was not easy to get a visa for Oman, but we who worked here had the right to have family visits now and then. Unfortunately, the families go back and tell friends and colleagues how nice Oman is. We also did so a couple of years ago after a short visit. When the dean of the faculty of medicine heard that, he said, "Please don't. It is the best-kept secret in the Middle East."

I received a Christmas card from a colleague. He wrote, "May your days be filled with harmony, your nights with welcome rest, may life reward day by day with nothing but the best." Rather beautiful, I thought.

Christmas day was celebrated with a boat trip. It was warm. A cloud passed before the sun. "A moment of blessing," my friend Nick said.

The Ascension of the Prophet and New Year

I shall now write about the ascension of the Prophet, which took place while he was alive. Therefore he could tell the public what he had experienced. I read the following in the Times of Oman newspaper of 31 December 1994, which this year incidentally was the day of his ascension:

"Muslims in all parts of the world cherish the day of the ascension of the Prophet, that day when he by night rode from the Holy Mosque of Mecca to the big mosque in Jerusalem and from there ascended to the skies. There are seven, and the Prophet (pbuh) visited them all. At that time the Prophet (pbuh) (*pbuh* means "peace be upon him") had problems. There were problems in the family with deaths, and he had been chased away by people throwing stones, people who did not want to be converted. Then descended an angel from the skies. The angel was the archangel Gabriel, who came with a *buraaq*, a white animal with two wings, smaller than a mule and bigger than a donkey. The Prophet (pbuh) now rode on this animal during the night to the Al Aqsaa Mosque in Jerusalem. The Prophet (pbuh) later said, 'The steps of the animal were so long as you could see with your eyes.' When he came to the mosque, he met a group of apostles. They asked him to lead a prayer, recognizing his prophetic qualities. Hereafter he rose to the skies. The archangel Gabriel accompanied him most of the way. After his miraculous ascension, he returned to Mecca that same night, God willing."

When he told this to people in Mecca the following day, there were some who did not believe him. It was tempting to assume he had been dreaming. Then God showed him Jerusalem for his inner eye, and he described in detail how Jerusalem looked. Some of those present had been there, and they found the description so detailed that all sceptics had to say, "He has really been there yesterday night," for everybody knew that otherwise he had not been to Jerusalem.

By this odd coincidence we were here at the evening of the ascension of the Prophet and New Year's Eve.

Chapter 2

In which one experiences the Holy Month of Ramadan and crosses the Wahiba Sands

Ramadan

His Majesty Sultan Qaboos has on the 27 Shaban 1415 AH (i.e., 24 January 1995) appointed a Moon Sighting Committee. The Minister for Islamic Affairs, who is also Minister of Justice, became chairman. Another member was the Grand Mufti of the Sultanate. The committee held its first meeting on 29 January. Hereafter there were regular meetings, so that it could be established when Ramadan begins. The worthy committee members do so by evaluating incoming observations. When two distinguished Omani men (not women) swear that they have seen the new moon, the committee decides that they will recommend to the Sultan that Ramadan begins. Here they do not need help from astronomers, since it is never or almost never overcast.

His Majesty decided that Ramadan, the Holy month, should begin 1 February 1995.

It is a problem to produce a calendar for the entire Arab world, since the new moon is seen at different times in the different countries. Therefore arrangements about meetings etc. are made in accordance with our Western calendar, which practically enough is printed together with the Arab calendar. It is planned that the Moon Sighting Committee shall meet again at the end of the month to decide when it should recommend to His

Majesty to end Ramadan. This point of time is important, because then the Sultan will declare that the following days shall become holidays. This period of joy is called *Eid al-Fitr*. If he is in a good mood, this period can last for a week, an extra holiday period. Then, for the Omanis, it is time to go on a binge and drink a lot of juice.

We, the Westerners, will be heading for the desert or into the mountains. The weather is still agreeable. You can sleep in the desert on camping beds. We once were camping with others in the Wahiba Sands. And we shall do it again. The camels then went around sniffing us, but without eating any of our daughter's blonde hair, like they did in Saudi Arabia, believing, I guess, that it was hay.

A Muslim is not allowed to eat or drink from sunrise to sunset during Ramadan. In the mosque they serve a glass of water and a date at sunset after the *Iftar* prayer. All Omanis are tired. They say it is because they do not eat or drink all day, the truth being they eat a lot every evening. There are big parties with plenty of food and juice for the closest family. Once we were guests at such a party. More than two hundred people. Families are big here.

Now, back at the Holy Ramadan. According to the Sultan's decree of 1 February 1995, working hours during Ramadan are restricted to the period from eight thirty a.m. to one thirty p.m. That should be manageable, we thought. The Western physicians use the quiet afternoons for preparing lectures and doing scientific work. During Ramadan, a number of patients, up to 90 per cent, do not turn up at their scheduled time. Like the airline companies, we try to solve the problem by overbooking. What can we do? We are visitors, not Omani citizens. It is their country. And in Arabia, time is not important. One can come some other day when one is not so tired.

There are a lot of things Muslims are not allowed to do during Ramadan (e.g., have sex with their wife [wives]). The women are not supposed to use makeup. And everybody must be good to those who need it. Here the Sultan takes the lead. According to a recent decree, in a number of shops he reduced the prices of all meat, even the finest beef to one rial per kilo, that price being valid for the whole month. I suppose he pays the difference. He has a big purse. His Majesty always thinks of the poorest.

We, the infidels, are not supposed to eat or drink while Muslims are watching. A girl from our daughter's school last year spent twenty-four hours in jail when she was seen chewing gum. We, the Westerners, permitted to buy alcoholic beverages, cannot buy any this month. For the first time, the Sultan has closed the liquor shops during Ramadan, probably as a gesture to the feelings of influential religious people in his entourage. They dislike that Westerners have access to buy the poisonous stuff, which like tobacco makes man lose his personality and dignity. The Prophet thought so too.

Ramadan is the Holy month, during which long ago the Koran started to be revealed to the Prophet. As one can see from what I have written above, we in some respects follow the Muslim calendar. The year is eleven days shorter than at home, and Ramadan takes place at different times from year to year. This, they say here, is because it would not be just if Ramadan occurred at the same time every year, because then the temperatures would be the same every year. The attentive reader may have perceived that the annual income would be higher when each month is shorter here than in Europe and America. This was and is the case in Saudi Arabia, but not here, where wages follow the Western calendar. The Omanis are practical and can adapt when it is opportune. The Prophet thought of everything.

There are exceptions from the strict rules of fasting: Women who have delivered recently or are menstruating do not have to fast, but can do it later, which they do. Nobody cheats. For many hospital patients fasting can be harmful, but they fast anyhow. We also do exercise tests on patients suspected of cardiovascular disease, although the patients are often very tired.

The good news during Ramadan is the fact that, as in previous years, shops reduce their prices. That is true even for car prices. For example, this year Mercedes has reduced their prices by 35 per cent, so a big luxury Mercedes car now costs the same here as a Mazda 123 at home. In order to make the purchase affordable, you can pay over two years, which is unusual for this country where people are used to paying cash. Also, during those two years, no interest is paid. Since interest is forbidden in the Holy Koran, it is obvious that interest cannot be paid during Ramadan. It is not easy to understand that it is possible to sell cars during the other months of the year.

This is an extract from today's newspaper on *20 Ramadan*, the subject being the battle of Badr: "The Prophet took part, and for the first time he was leader in a battle. Before the battle he was praying for his troops. They were three hundred; the enemy had a thousand warriors. 'O God Almighty, help them, for if they are annihilated, Thou shalt no more be worshipped in future.' He started, like Montgomery before the battle of El Alamein, by inducing self respect by discipline. He went along the rows of men and pushed those back who were not in line. Exercise. And he explained cleverly: 'Do not move, do not break the lines. When the enemy is close, but not before, use your arrows, when he is closer use the stones you have collected and placed at your feet, thereafter throw your lances and spears, and only at last use your sword.'"

And the famous *dictum* of the Prophet: "God has prescribed to behave well in every matter; so if you kill, kill in a nice way." As everybody knows, he won the battle.

The moon has now become so small that the Moon Sighting Committee must meet soon. We think this day may be the last one of Ramadan. People are still fasting, but after the *Iftar prayer* tonight or tomorrow it might be the end of the Holy month of Ramadan. The month for self-control and meditation and gratefulness for the creative power of Allah seems to be over soon, as judged from the size of the moon. It is rumoured that His Majesty (HM) Sultan Qaboos has decided we shall all have five days off.

It has been decided that the Moon Sighting Committee shall meet tonight. At last the night is arriving, the night over all nights, the night of blessing. During this night all your prayers are equivalent to your prayers of eighty-three years. No surprise everybody stays awake tonight, as did the Prophet many years ago. This night is the most peaceful night of the year, almost like Christmas Eve.

We shall miss Ramadan.

Wahiba Sands

We started early afternoon. We all stop working early during Ramadan, and this was the last weekend of Ramadan. Although we observe Ramadan, we departed. It was still cool, twenty-two Celsius in the morning and thirty-two Celsius in the afternoon. We were nine persons in four cars, all filled up with petrol, water, and food. A last stop in Minitrib, off again, and we were in the desert, the Wahiba Sands, which we had earlier seen on the horizon and heard a lot about. We started on a wrong track and got stuck. Good exercise, as Konrad said. He is German. At long last we found the track which would lead us southwards through the unique landscape on to the sand dunes at the sea 150 kilometres farther on. We all wondered if our abilities to drive in sand would suffice, and whether we would have accidents. Did we have enough water? Did we have enough petrol? One needs quite a lot when stuck.

I was driving our Land Rover Discovery, a reliable car in the desert, although not so good as the Toyota Land Cruiser. At the beginning, I was satisfied with myself. Everything was going well, and then, suddenly we were stuck in soft sand. A moment of deficient concentration while driving uphill. We were the last of the four cars.

Well, we knew our leader, Bengt, who is a Swede, would come back with sand ladders, expertise, and good spirits. We started digging out the car. Bengt and the others did not come. Our daughter went to the top of the hill. Nothing to see. Quiet, no sound apart from the whistling of the wind. Sand and sand. We were sweating, but we had fifty litres of water in the car, so we would probably not die from lack of water. The others might be stuck further on. It turned out they were stuck almost at the same spot, so they could help each other. Finally we all got loose. We understood it is unwise to drive alone in the desert. People have done that and regretted it. Some have died.

First night out: champagne before dinner. Wine accompanied delicious food. We were far away from civilization, and we got to know each other better. We talked about driving in sand. This first day all cars were stuck a couple of times. We needed to practice. Having a four-wheel-drive car is not enough. We had, however, managed quite well, and we were in high spirits, but that would not last. The night was beautiful. We slept on our camping beds covered by our Bedouin blankets to protect us from the dew.

The next day started well. The weather was pleasant, not hot. The colours in the desert are beautiful in the early morning light. Off we went, getting stuck a couple of times, but we were learning all the time. Once when my car got stuck, one of the doors was open. I was digging. A camel suddenly had his head in the car trying to find something to eat. No human being could be seen apart from my family. It is rather cosy with camels. There is something soothing about them. The camels of the Wahiba Sands are of a particularly refined kind. They walk around slowly with half-closed eyes, heads arrogantly backwards. That is because they know all the hundred names of Allah. No human being knows more than ninety-nine of them. Some camels can be used for racing, and there are stories of poor Bedouins who became millionaires overnight because they sold a camel at a price corresponding to the most expensive Rolls Royce. I had obsessions about camels and cars in frontal crashes on top of sand hills where you cannot see far. You have to drive fast uphill. You follow old tracks, and so do those driving the other way. Bengt and Ulla have a Mitsubishi Pajero, with a 3-litre engine, broad tires, and a working compass. Konrad, our German colleague, professor of pharmacology, and his wife have a Land Rover Discovery like ours, a 3.5-litre engine. Konrad's son and daughter have a Mitsubishi Pajero without impressive power, but reliable.

We had reduced the pressure of the tires of all the cars when we entered the desert. The cars performed well, did not break down. A hole in a tube or a deficient driving belt can be disastrous in the desert. In those days, GPS systems were not installed in our cars, so it might be difficult to retrieve our cars if abandoned. Konrad had ample supplies of spare parts, so we were not nervous. The problem is often the driver, not the car. Even experienced drivers can make mistakes. We got proof of that on the third day, but we did not know that when we were camping in the evening of the second day, dining on grilled beef with baked potatoes and Australian red wine of superior quality. We slept well.

We were camping at the bottom of the big sand dunes in the south of the Wahiba Sands. Before we went off in the morning, we had visitors. A Bedouin was on his way to the market not far away, accompanied by his veiled wife and some of their children. He had two small goats on his pickup, and asked if we were interested in buying them. It is well known that you celebrate *Eid al-Fitr* by cutting the throat of a goat and braise it in sand for six hours. Delicious with juice, the man said. "No, thank you." We had enough food. We were alone in the desert once again, except for a Bedouin woman far away. She went at a constant speed uphill and downhill without problems, effortlessly, not snorting and groaning like we were.

At first everything went well. Correct gear. Speed, forty-five hundred revolutions per minute. The first part was uphill. Bengt was waving. We should come closer. We did, stopping five hundred meters farther on, on firm ground after a hill top, as recommended. Konrad, whom after some glasses the evening before I had persistently called cognac, came up to our side. The others were nowhere to be seen. Bengt and Ulla went on.

We heard the sound of an engine, which stopped. No sounds. Silence. I went on foot to the edge of a big hole. Fifty meters down was Bengt and Ulla's car half-buried in sand. We stopped the small Pajero with Konrad's children before they made the same mistake. Here we were, three cars on the edge of a big hole, one car at the bottom of it. Bengt, our experienced leader, had been driving where there were no tracks, something he had warned us against doing. It was very steep, a slope of sixty degrees. To our relief we saw them climbing out of the car, presumably unhurt. Relief. Luckily he had hit the edge perpendicularly, so his car had not turned over. We had heard about similar accidents with fatal outcomes.

After recovering from the shock, we began to think of how we could recover Bengt's car from the giant desert hole. We climbed down. We tried with sand ladders after digging. We could not get it up; the slopes were too steep. It was hot. We talked about abandoning the car, driving on in three cars, in order to rescue Bengt's car later, knowing it might be difficult to find it, but hoping we could retrace the spot with others. There were stories about cars lost forever.

Then, a miracle. Allah sent us a Bedouin. He passed by, saw the empty cars, and wondered where we were. He stopped his car, went to the edge, and saw us at the bottom of the giant hole. He came down, stretched out his right hand, and got the car keys from Bengt. He did not speak a word of English, but it was obvious he offered to help. He almost emptied the tires of air, placed sand ladders in front of the car, and drove it at high revolutions out of this sand trap at the bottom of the hole. It was Allah who lifted the car up from the hole right in front of our eyes. The Bedouin drove slowly on the slopes of the hole, forming a twisted path along the sides. Finally he was back on the edge. The car was not damaged, and everybody was happy. We thanked this gentle, worthy Bedouin. We offered him money. He declined. Then we offered him fresh fruit for his children. He accepted that. He had five of them, and judging from his age and apparent virility, he might have more in due time.

Bedouins are masters of sand driving. They can "read" the sand, see where the sand is soft and where it is hard. Bedouins often use sand tires, a special type of broad "balloon tires" in which the air pressure is only one third of the pressure we use for our cars.

After the shock, we speeded up and drove to the beach as planned. It was low tide, as Bengt said it would be. We were driving on hard, fossil sand in beautiful formations to the left, the sea to the right. Occasional fishermen. Soon there was almost no petrol left, a serious problem. We were driving in the periphery of the desert on a road marked on our map. Luckily we had a British military map. Maps are otherwise forbidden here. They are military secrets. War is not a theoretical possibility here, but something which can become real at short notice.

I stopped a Toyota pickup in order to enquire how to reach the nearest petrol station. The Toyota was driven by a seven-year-old boy. He had had a recent thorough haircut and was almost bald. This was a sign that he had gone through his circumcision ceremony. Apparently he was now a man. He drove nicely, standing up to reach the pedals, but it was not easy for him to look through the windscreen. His grandfather sat next to him, apparently blind. Perhaps it was good he was not the driver. Blindness is common here. There is a lot to do for ophthalmologists. We have quite a number of them at the university. Bengt told us about the day he had assisted a Bedouin when his car was stuck in the sand near the sea. The Bedouin asked Bengt to position himself behind the steering wheel of his car, which was rather unusual, because normally the natives consider themselves better drivers than we are. The explanation was that this man was totally blind. He used to drive with an open window so that he could hear the waves when driving from one place on the coast to another. I shall be more careful in future stopping cars here. Perhaps blind drivers in the desert are not uncommon. Certainly blindness, the end result of trachoma (a bacterial infection of the eye), is common here.

When we returned home after having visited the most needed petrol station, it began to rain. The children were up late playing with water in small pools at their houses. Some were seen lying down in the water. The youngest had never experienced rain before.

Wahiba Sands left an impression never to be forgotten. Allow me to quote from Wilfred Thesiger's *Arabian Sands,* saying about the desert Bedouins, "No man can live this life and emerge unchanged. He will carry, however faint, the imprint of the desert, the brand which marks the nomad; and he will have within him the yearning to return, weak or insistent according to his nature. For this cruel land can cast a spell which no temperate clime can match."

Chapter 3

In which one discusses childbirth and polygamy

Childbirth

The population is increasing rapidly in this country, like in other Arab countries. It is said that for the time being there are a little more than one million Omanis and more than half a million expatriates. The Omanis have many children. The families are big. The expatriates, mostly Indians, are not supposed to breed during their first two years here. If they do they are sent back. They can only stay if they have a job (i.e., a sponsor). Many are worried that the population of Oman is rising so quickly there will not be enough work for everybody. But the Sultan says cleverly, "How can one say we have too many children when we in this country have six hundred thousand Indians?" The statistics at the university say that on average each Omani woman will have five to six children, and elsewhere figures of seven to eight children have been mentioned. It should be remembered that infertility is as common here as in the West. Since the number of childbirths follows a Gaussian curve of distribution, it is not uncommon to meet Omani women with twenty children.

An Omani friend has eighteen brothers and sisters from the same mother. All had a higher education abroad, and they are all doing well, some of them having very good jobs here. Our friend is, by the way, very modern. He has only one wife and only five children. The latest they gave away to the wife's sister. She had no children of her own and could not have any. They all felt this solution to her problem was better than adopting a child whose genetic background was unknown. The Norwegians did the same a thousand years ago.

The girls start early here, are often married at the age of twelve, after having their first menstruation. For some it is also the last one, because they are pregnant or breastfeeding until their climacteric (menopause). It is also well known here in Oman that lactation is used as a method of preventing pregnancy. His Majesty calls it "birth spacing." He does not tell the Omanis they should not have many children, but that there should be longer time between the births out of consideration for the health of the women.

The Sultan's view on this matter is supported by our wise professor of paediatrics, who knows all about the disasters following campaigns of milk powder given to babies: diarrhoea and other infectious diseases, which can be lethal, because the immunity of the babies is reduced when lactation is abolished. At the main entrance of our hospital there are two posters made by students. One is a picture of two cows, one saying to the other, "There is an alarming new trend among cows. Some want their calves to have human milk. Isn't that ridiculous?" The other poster is a slogan: "Breast Milk. The Instant Food."

The Holy Koran says, "The mothers shall give suck to their offspring for two complete years." Not long ago a book was published in the Sultanate about the blessings of lactation. It is a thorough summary of an extensive work the purpose of which was to encourage Omani women to lactate longer. The first chapter has the impressive heading: "The Wonder Drug." One of the recommendations of the book is breastfeeding for two years, which previously was common here. Other recommendations are making sure the mothers start lactation half an hour after delivery; and not separating the child from the mother, allowing the mother to be with her child twenty-four hours per day. Perhaps we in the West could learn something here? In this way the health authorities try to improve public health. The campaign has begun to work. Infant mortality due to diarrhoea is being reduced after milk powder was substituted by breast milk. The women here also know very well that breastfeeding prevents pregnancy.

Recently I examined a twenty-five-year-old woman. She had had nine children and probably had a number of years ahead during which she could please her husband by having even more children. Her medical problem was low-back pain and fatigue. Her body weight was forty-five kilograms. There was no serious medical problem, but it is of course a problem that her husband is not interested in prevention. Nine children at the age of twenty-five years a bit much. In Europe we had similar problems with multiparity a hundred years ago and earlier. One of my great-great-grandmothers had twenty-four children with one husband. They were wealthy, could afford to have wet nurses. No long lactation periods. Therefore, twenty-four children.

That is probably almost the maximum number of children a woman can have, unless she has twins or triplets once or twice. Sometimes we hear that having children is normal for normal women, but both our gynaecologists and we who are not experts can see it might be too much.

We have heard stories about women who accept that their husbands take another wife. It might be a relief. Funny enough, there are no stories of women taking another man (polyandry). That would be illegal. It seems it is very rare that wives are unfaithful, but that is of course difficult to know. If it does happen, she will be punished. In Saudi Arabia, they know how to deal with this problem. The woman is stoned. Thereby a repeated crime is avoided. In later years, the old fashioned way of throwing stones by hand has been abandoned. Now they use a truck which empties its load of stones directly on her head, the only part of her body not buried in sand. Consequently, the men no longer have shoulder pain from throwing stones.

We never hear that Omani men are interested in prevention, which is allowed here in contrast to certain catholic countries. It is, however, said that Omani women are very interested, and there is a rumour that Sultan Qaboos has set aside some money for prevention, but so far nobody has seen that money. Unfortunately, people here cannot pay themselves, it is said.

An Omani man may have thirty to forty children, if he has more than one wife. It is a sign of wealth. Our daughter, fifteen years old, was recently driven home from school by a young Omani man of eighteen. He stayed in different hotels and had neither work nor education. Dad paid for everything, including his new BMW. This young chap had thirty brothers and sisters. Not many have such a man as a father.

Delivery normally (in nine out of ten cases) takes place at a hospital. Often the mother of the pregnant women is present, assisting if needed, because she knows what it is all about. The husband does not. She can tell her daughter that walking is sometimes a good idea. The coming father would not know that. Only 5 per cent of the deliveries in Oman take place by caesarean section, a low figure compared to Northern Europe. It is not my impression that complications are frequent.

Omani women do not make much fuss. Having a baby is something quite normal, not a disease. A woman has a baby now and then. We had a female patient recently. She had delivered fourteen times, every time at home, without assistance of any kind, without help from any human being. That was confirmed by her sister, who spoke English well. Eleven of the fourteen children survived. That, she thought, was fine; none had died immediately after being born.

Omani children are quiet. Unusually quiet. You practically never see a crying Omani child, perhaps because their mothers hold them tight from morning to evening. Often the child falls asleep when carried by the mother. It is said that cot death is rare here. We are not sure. Statistics are not so good in Oman, but perhaps we should take up our children a little more at home. Even the older children are quieter here than at home. Stress is rare. Time is not important; they have plenty of time here, and they are not being disturbed by mobile phones, radios, and television, unlike in the West, where it seems children and adults prefer the company of their cell phone to human relations, a dangerous trend.

Polygamy

One day I had a patient from the VIP department. Such a thing does exist. People are not equal ... or some are more equal than others. He was the director at one of the ministries, fifty-eight years old, a man who was used to commanding. He had expressed a wish to have his heart examined at rest and during exercise. We obeyed. After the test, I told him everything was normal. He became so happy and enthusiastic. He kissed me on both cheeks, as it is the custom here, something I never tried before – by a man. Now he could take another wife, marry again, this time a younger wife, a wife number two. It is important that number two is young, in order to avoid that the wives become old at the same time.

We have heard about a Muslim man who forgot this golden rule. He had four wives of identical age. He had married them all at the same time when they were fifteen, so they became old at the same time, and he made a fool of himself, became the laughingstock of the village.

My VIP patient kept thanking me at repeated visits the following days, but I said again and again that he should thank Allah, I only being a tool in the hands of Allah. Before being discharged, he came to my clinic, gave me his business card, and asked me to contact him if I had a problem. That I have not done – yet.

If a man has more than one wife, he must treat them equally according to the Holy Koran. No preferences are allowed. You are not supposed to give a gold bracelet to one of your wives and not to the others. That may become expensive. On our way to the fishing village Seeb, we once saw two completely identical villas, both with large, completely identical gardens. They belong to a rich man with two wives. When he comes home from work, one day he goes to the right and the next day to the left. Furniture, kitchens, bedrooms, etc. are identical, the only difference being the wives. More than one wife is unusual here, in contrast to Saudi Arabia, but I have met Omani men with four wives. For those men, Volvo has produced an extra long sedan, with six doors and two rows of back seats, so the wives do not have to sit tight, but there is a problem if all the children are supposed to accompany their parents. A motorcar with twenty to thirty seats is not yet available.

If, after having read this, somebody feels inclined to convert to Islam in order to enjoy the pleasures of polygamy, I can only say it is not easy to convert. And then there is something else: all the men in Arabia I have met who have more than one wife are tired. They must share their wealth and time on a basis of equality. A Muslim man is not expected to love each of his wives equally. Love is something that is up to Allah.

By the way, mutual sympathy is not important for your choice of a wife. As the Prophet said, "You may marry a woman for the following reasons: her fortune; her family background; her beauty; her religiousness. You should, however, always marry a religious woman, and you shall be satisfied."

There are many problems associated with having more wives. What do you do when you are going away, and can afford to bring only one of your wives? Perhaps you do not have the new long Volvo. So you draw lots. If fate decides you shall bring one of your wives, who for the time being you are not satisfied with, you do not have to bring her, but you cannot bring one of the others. Even if you do not like her now, you must have sex with her as with your other wives.

Allah's messenger, the Prophet Mohammed, was permitted by Allah to have nine wives. He was extremely righteous, dividing his time carefully between the nine wives. Once one of them became old and less attractive. She was afraid of being repudiated. She then offered her day and the following night to one of the younger wives. The Prophet only agreed to this arrangement if all the wives agreed. They did. Thereby she avoided divorce and could stay in the family. All this and more too can be read in a book written by two Westerners who converted to Islam, Abu Ameennah Philips and Jameelah Jones. The book is titled *Polygamy in Islam*. It deals with the big problem Western single mothers have: it can be difficult to find a man when you are divorced after having been married for many years.

This problem does not exist in Arab countries. I had a Western female colleague, a doctor who is a divorcee with three children. She said to me when I suggested a new marriage, "But they are all taken." An Arab woman has better chances to remarry. She can be a second or third wife. She will be allotted three consecutive days with her husband after the wedding. If she had been a virgin she would have had seven days. After that she will have night duty like the others.

We often discuss the relationship between the wives in polygamous marriages. There are stories of friendship and strong family feelings, like between sisters. There are also stories of severe jealousy. A young man of twenty-seven had confidence in me because I had helped his mother with a health problem. He told me about his neighbour, who loved his wife. Unfortunately, she could not have children. After many years, they decided he should marry once again. He found a very young wife who blessed him with a number of children. All children were brought up by the first wife, whom they regarded as their mother. The second wife was busy becoming or being pregnant. The two women were very good friends, and it was a happy family.

The young man then told me of himself. He married five years ago. His wife could not have children either. They were sad about this. He loved his wife too. They had now agreed that he should take another wife because it is so nice with children, and the local gynaecologists had not been able to help. Hopefully, it is not a case of male infertility.

I remember a case from the waiting room. A lady comforted her fellow wife, who could not get pregnant. In this country she then is not a real woman. She only becomes a real woman when she delivers a baby boy. If she is sterile she can be returned to her parents in case the husband refuses to keep her. No children. What a shame. Or she can become very poor if the husband dies. Widows without children inherit very little.

Homosexuality

Sterility is a problem that our gynaecologists try to solve, spending a lot of time on this. On the other hand, they are not overburdened with abortions. Abortion is not an option here and is forbidden, unless there are medical reasons. One gets the children one must have.

Unless of course the husband is homosexual. Then there will be no babies. If the husband has this problem, the wife has the right to leave him. Male homosexuality is accepted here on the Batinah coast as long as the man is not the receiving part. If you belong to the latter group of homosexuals, you are despicable. One can often but not always identify a homosexual man by looking at his nails. The nail surroundings are beautifully decorated with henna. Painting of the eye surroundings is, however, not a sign of homosexuality. It is often used, and I have seen it many times. They say it is an ancient tradition. It looks nice, and it is believed the eye makeup is disinfecting, preventing eye infections. However, some of the men who used it earlier were intoxicated because it contained bismuth.

Whether homosexuality is more frequent in Arabia than elsewhere has been discussed over the years. In the mountains, homosexuality seems less frequent than in the capital area where we live. The explanation we got from a medical student who was asked by his professor why it seems to be so. The student replied, "We shoot them; that is why."

Unfortunately, it is not easy to talk with Omanis about their family affairs. It is private and embarrassing. We have learned never to ask how their wife (wives) is (are).

Chapter 4

In which one discusses health and disease and tells about an episode of unusual rainy weather

Health and Disease

One should know a little about the health problems of a people in order to understand their problems. But for Oman, it is not easy, because the medico-statistical information in this county is sparse. The Ministry of Health publishes a yearbook, but I realized evaluation of the information given in the book should be one of scepticism when I heard the following story. Our expert in infectious diseases had produced his annual information about the incidence and prevalence of AIDS among hospital patients. He sent it to the Ministry. When the yearbook appeared, the official number of AIDS cases in the country was only half of what he had reported to the authorities for the university hospital alone.

A British/Polish couple, Joe and his wife, arrived here at the same time as we did, so we are puzzled by the same things. Joe is an experienced gynaecologist. That might be difficult to believe when hearing that he spent most of his professional life as a gynaecologist in the British army and ended as lieutenant colonel. He claims he was very busy because so many wives of officers needed his assistance. The British army has been all over the globe. "Join the army and see the world." We often discuss whether the many deliveries of Omani women unfavourably influence female health. More specifically, I asked him whether the many childbirths per woman here do increase the occurrence of female incontinence. "No, on the contrary." He believes incontinence here is less frequent than in the West. He knows why: because the women here since childhood are used to squatting when they sit down resting. Men do too. That strengthens the pelvic floor. In the West, we all sit on chairs.

The famous author Wilfred Thesiger describes in *Arabian Sands* an expedition to the interior of the country. Apart from the usual native entourage of Omanis, a European man was present. He went a little aside to pass urine, standing up as we normally do in the West. One of the Arabs said, "Is he ill, since he cannot sit down?" Squatting is so common here that when an Omani man or woman from the interior encounters a Western toilet in the Capital Area, he or she often sits on the toilet squatting. If squatting prevents urinary incontinence it is indeed interesting, perhaps an example that we in the West unnecessarily and unwillingly undermine our health.

In Europe and America we damage our feet using bad but expensive shoes, which press our toes together, resulting in painful hammertoes and corns. Such maltreatment of feet does not exist here. Everybody uses sandals or moves around barefoot with the result that the feet of the Omanis are healthy with a straight big toe and feet that can walk far. His Majesty has nice feet. He is of course always dressed in Omani clothing with a turban, *kunjar* (an Omani knife), and sandals. He is always thusly photographed, never in European clothes. His turban is of a refined pattern and colour, only to be used by the Royal Family.

When top officials from the West visit, they are welcomed by His Majesty. His Majesty is wearing sandals. The guests sit in jacket, tie, and black shoes producing pain in their feet, sweating and looking uncomfortable in the Omani heat. Even though the feet of the Omanis can walk far, the Omanis do not walk much in the hot season. But from November until April there are possibilities. Exercise prevents bone loss and can even increase bone mass. We do not know exactly if osteoporosis is as frequent here as at home. When you see elderly women in the mountains carrying heavy burdens on their head with a straight back like they have done for thousands of years, one might presume that osteoporosis is rare in the interior, where people walk a lot. Here in the Capital Area, osteoporosis is not rare, and the number of operations for hip fracture is as high as in Europe, the number of inhabitants considered. It is believed the sedentary lifestyle of this region might be responsible for development of not only osteoporosis but diabetes and coronary heart disease.

Modern Omanis have cars. Many families have a number of cars. Our hospital director, who is Omani, has five: a big Mercedes for himself, a four-wheel drive for the desert, a smaller sedan for his wife, and two for the grown-up children. Driving cars and walking little tend to result in bone loss and osteoporosis. This habit of not exercising comes from the West, something we should not be proud of. The young people here, however, now seem to be becoming interested in sports and fitness.

Concerning my friend Joe, he came to England from Poland after the war, and therefore has a slight accent. His name is in fact Joseph, named after the brother of Marie Curie. He was a Polish surgeon. Joe's father, also a surgeon, worked with Joseph Curie when he was young.

Joe for the time being does not have much to do. He explains. If a woman with a gynaecological problem wants to see a gynaecologist, she needs first to persuade her husband to let her go to the hospital, which is far away. Then the man will have to accompany her. The male gynaecologist must then have the permission from both to let him examine her in this "no-touch region." Also, they have their own shyness to fight against. It is not surprising that the diagnosis is sometimes made too late, so late that treatment is impossible.

It is written in the Holy Koran that you shall wash all natural orifices and their surroundings before prayer. And you do. The Omanis are clean and do not smell from sweat in spite of difficulties with access to water and the hot climate. There is water at the mosque. The hygiene is extended to the autos. His Majesty has decided that no car in Oman should be dirty, so people wash their cars again and again, even in the wadis. That rule of car washing creates problems when you return home from the desert, and the guard at the hospital entrance asks you to turn back in order to have your car washed before you are allowed to enter the hospital premises and your home. Car washing is not the first thing you think of after days in the rough nature of Oman.

Water keeps diseases away. That has been known for centuries. But water can also be dangerous. Mosquitoes infected with malaria parasites love non-streaming water, like the water in the wadi pools. Therefore we keep away from fresh water, although we know malaria is not common in this country. Malaria is so rare here that we do not take malaria prophylaxis. But we have mosquito nets at home. It is said that mosquitoes only sting at the end of the day at dusk, during the blue hour. Our specialist in infectious diseases has promised to treat and cure us if we should be unluckily infected with malaria. Whether he can is another matter. It would be unfortunate if the first malaria attack came after we had returned to Northern Europe. Then you cannot be sure malaria is the first diagnosis the European physician would think of in case of fever and shivering fits. Not all physicians have imagination, but imagination is together with faculty of combination most important for physicians.

The other day we had a shock. One of our Omani receptionists, Mohammed, died from acute cerebral malaria, which was neither diagnosed nor treated in time. He had been in East Africa on vacation and had been infected with the much-feared aggressive type of malaria which affects the brain and is resistant to all types of treatments. He and his doctor thought he had influenza. He died in fewer than twenty-four hours after his return from Zanzibar.

In one month, this type of malaria has killed 724 people in Bangladesh according to official statistics, so the real number is probably higher. This aggressive type of malaria is also seen in India, where hundreds have died during the last few weeks. The parasites kill more people than the much-feared Ebola virus from Zaire, according to newspapers. Mohammed died at age thirty-nine, leaving behind a wife and three small children. He was buried the same day, as is normally the case here. No ceremony. Down into the earth quickly, and then immediately up into the heavens where everything is definitely better than down here, they say. Some flu.

Tuberculosis, in some parts of the Third World an even bigger problem than malaria, does not create big problems here where most people are vaccinated.

We have lately heard much about the plague in India. All flights between Oman and the subcontinent have been cancelled for weeks. Our experts did not worry much. The plague has been common in India for many years, and the disease can be treated. Regarding the size of the Indian population, a couple hundred cases is nothing to worry about, they say. The Emirates used the plague to discharge those of the Indians who after vacation in India could not return to the Emirates due to the cancelled flights. They failed to turn up and were therefore discharged without pay. In the UAE (United Arab Emirates) there are more Indians than Arabs, so the authorities try to get rid of some of them when possible.

The Omanis in the mountains are often athletic and fit, not the least the women. In the cities and in the Dhofar region (the southern part of the country), obesity is common. Females being overweight are regarded as beautiful. And it is a sign of wealth, a sign that one can afford to pay others to do corporal work. It was like that in Europe years ago. I thought of the Russian writer Leo Tolstoy, who described how in Tsarist Russia it was a sign of wealth if a man had long nails. Then everybody knew he did not have to work.

According to online sources, life expectancy has risen from approximately 58 years in 1980 to around 67 years in 1993. Interestingly, also in this part of the world women live longer than men in spite of many childbirths. They live around one year longer on average.

The explanation why people live longer has something to do with neonatal deaths. They have decreased from sixty-four to twenty-three deaths per thousand deliveries of live children during that period. Very good, if it is true. It probably is. Certain diseases (e.g., polio, measles, diphtheria, and tuberculosis) are becoming obsolete due to vaccination campaigns, now being so rare that is difficult to demonstrate them to the students. Even leprosy, which in earlier days was common here, is now rare. If diagnosed it is now treatable.

AIDS is being diagnosed increasingly often. A wealthy Omani man was admitted to our hospital, accompanied by three of his adult sons. He had three wives and a lot of children. He clearly had active AIDS and was almost terminal. Careful interviewing revealed that he sometimes went to Dubai where he had lady friends. We agreed with his sons not to reveal the diagnosis to the patient. If we had done so he would have accused one or more of the wives of having infected him with this terrible disease. Then she or they would have been repudiated. It turned out two of the wives were infected and more of the children. The man died soon after. Polygamy is not without risks.

There are also problems with the eye disease trachoma. Trachoma is a serious, contagious eye disease which is common in certain areas of the country. In the north, up to 30 per cent of the population has it. If untreated it leads to blindness. If diagnosed in time it can be cured, so diagnosis has high priority. Now I understand why I see so many elderly people who are completely blind.

The surgical diseases are not more exotic here than at home, and operations are done if the patient agrees. That is not always the case. "One shall not intermingle with the creative power of Allah. Neither should one let them take some of your blood [blood sampling]. One could lose some of one's soul." The worst is that many husbands refuse to let our surgeons operate on their wives. The wives are not asked. Many women have died because of this. However, Western medicine has begun to play its role. Only in elderly people does one see traces of the old way of treating pain, namely large scars after burning with glowing sticks of hot iron. I can hear the sizzling sound in my inner ear. One type of pain coming from biliary colic or something else was replaced by another type of pain. I often thought I'd tried something like that. I had acupuncture because of prolonged sinusitis. My old pain disappeared for half an hour because of the new pain coming from the acupuncture needle.

Organ transplants are not yet done in this country. Omanis travel to India, only a couple of hours away by air. There you have access to a multitude of donor kidneys, legal or illegal. Usually the operation itself goes well. It is said that the Indian surgeons are good. Unfortunately, when they return home, one third of the operated patients discover they are infected with AIDS. Whether it is all due to blood transfusions or whether the transplanted kidney comes from an infected individual is difficult to know. It might be a good idea to start doing kidney transplants in Oman. I will tell the Sultan if I ever meet him.

The latest news is that we have opened a section for bone marrow transplants, used in case of certain haematological diseases. Earlier those patients, many of them children, were sent to London for treatment. It is cheaper to treat them here, and now we have the expertise.

Many obese patients in Oman die young from cardiovascular diseases. There is another problem for fat Omanis, which is well described in the medical literature, but new to me: Sleep apnoea, often a problem for obese people. This is a condition dominated by snoring and difficulties in breathing, often caused by too much fat in the throat. It may become serious. The oxygen saturation of the blood may become dangerously reduced. If the coronary arteries of the heart are narrow or the arteries leading blood to the brain are narrow, disasters may occur, such as a coronary infarction or a stroke. Patients with sleep apnoea can even die during their sleep. It becomes dangerous to sleep. I did not realize how dangerous until I started doing laboratory investigations. In our department we have a sleep lab, the only one in the country, in which we can monitor changes in a variety of parameters.

One of my Omani friends had sleep apnoea. I realized that at a meeting when I heard him snoring loudly in the midst of an interesting discussion. Then I saw that he had a kind of empty expression on his face while others were speaking. These patients can sleep with their eyes open. They often fall asleep during the day after having slept badly during the night. They may even fall asleep while driving their car. So did our friend. One day he almost killed a little girl playing in front of her house because he fell asleep behind the steering wheel. He then accepted my offer to sleep one night in our sleep laboratory. He was snoring. It turned out that he had severe cardiac arrhythmias: ventricular fibrillation and periods of something even worse, which had the potential of leading to cardiac arrest. I persuaded him to seek treatment. He agreed and has now lost weight and during the night he is breathing through a device (a CPAP machine), increasing the pressure of inspired air. He is now doing well, although his heart condition made it necessary later to have a cardiac bypass, which was done here successfully.

It can be seen that overweight may be dangerous. Sleeping is also potentially dangerous. It is said that among the many car accidents in this country, around one-fourth are caused by the driver falling asleep, often because of sleep apnoea.

I have a new colleague who is an otologist, a specialist in ear-nose-and-throat diseases. His name is Rahman. He is clever; a good doctor. Like me he likes to do things he has not tried before. In this case it was an operation on the soft palate. It appeared not to be difficult, so we did not regard this operation, his first of its kind, as experimental. It was well described in the books. The patient in question was a male, obese patient who snored so loudly that his wife did not want to sleep in the same room. That he did not like. In the sleep lab he was snoring so loudly that we could hear him through three closed doors when we tested him at night. Our lab technicians could not read their newspaper.

Our readings were scary. This gentleman needed treatment. He was in favour of a swift solution to his problem. He did not like the idea of waiting until he had lost twenty-five kilograms. He would be operated on by Dr Rahman. Before the operation, this patient had long periods of reduced blood oxygen, when we tested him. After the operation he had none. I told Rahman he had cured the patient.

He replied modestly, "It is not me, it is Allah."

It is nice to be pioneering, and it is nice to be able to help your fellow man, who would otherwise have had no help, but you do not have to be proud of it.

Food may taste good and may be healthy, but food in excessive amounts combined with too little exercise may be life threatening because then the body weight goes up, and obesity is dangerous. Losing weight here is difficult because it is difficult to exercise in the heat, so one must eat less. In the interior, they eat a great deal of dates and rice. Omani cuisine is not characterized by the same refinement as Lebanese, Persian, or Turkish cuisine. However, they eat fruits (e.g., limes, grapefruits, oranges and Omani mini bananas, which taste better than other bananas). Therefore, we do not believe vitamin deficiencies are common here, but we do not know exactly. It may be that vitamin D deficiency can be seen in elderly women, like in Saudi Arabia, due to moderate sun exposure and food lacking in vitamin D. People here who want to lose weight eat fruit, which is diverse and good.

Elsewhere in this book I discuss lime and gin and tonic. Here is the true story about why the British navy for centuries gave each sailor an allowance of rum. It all comes from a young physician serving in His British Majesty's navy. The young doctor had observed that the seamen got scurvy after having been at sea for six weeks. The food was dull. He had noticed that their symptoms disappeared when they came ashore in Jamaica, where they consumed large quantities of citrus fruits. He wrote a scientific article about his observation, claiming there was something healthy in citrus fruits, but the article was not accepted. He thereafter published his article privately, paying for the publication with his own money. His family was wealthy. The French read the article, but did not believe him. But the British navy introduced fruit juice and fresh citrus fruits (lime, which they got from India and Oman). These fruits last long. Lime is acid, but is more easily swallowed when taken with rum, sometimes with a little sugar added. This was the story behind the rum rations in the British navy, a tradition which lasted until the Second World War.

Some believe the reason the British Empire comprised one-fifth of the surface of the globe was lime. When a small British frigate encountered a big French frigate, it was not afraid of starting a naval action. All the British seamen and officers were fit and ready for combat. Many of those onboard French naval ships were not, lying down with scurvy (vitamin C deficiency), and therefore the French navy often could not fight well.

Diabetes with or without complications is very common in Oman, whatever the cause. It is said that in certain areas, one-third of the population has diabetes. We often see diabetics at the hospital. Many have heart problems. Coronary heart disease is not uncommon at age thirty. It does not help that cigarette smoking is becoming popular among youngsters. They now smoke on the streets, something said to be quite new. The Sultan has not yet introduced indirect taxes. If he does, cigarettes might be a good place to start. Perhaps Europe can help. Taxation is something we in Europe, particularly in North Europe, know about. Not long ago the British Finance Minister was visiting. He was supposed to give advice on how to reduce the budget deficiency of the state. We guess there will be a reduction in wages and fees. We do hope the great man will not suggest to the Sultan to introduce VAT (value-added tax), or whisper the words "direct taxes." Last time somebody said that, it was categorically rejected.

Rain

At the beginning of April we drove 350 kilometres through mountains and low-lying country to the Indian Ocean farther south and were stuck in the sand near the fishing village Al Askara. Three off-roaders of the best kind. Our saviour was a seventeen-year-old Arab boy. He probably waited for somebody to get stuck. He was pleased to help. It seemed he expected this to happen. He knew the sand was soft where most Westerners preferred to drive, because there were tracks. Perhaps he had made the tracks himself? It reminded me of the pilot we had in Skælskør, Denmark, where my parents had a summer house. The man, Arthur, was piloting ships through the narrow Skælskør Inlet. His problem was that there were too few ships, too little money to be made, and too little to do. The days were long. He was waiting for a ship at his little harbour. Then a yacht from Copenhagen approached. Arthur sat there smoking his pipe, and was very calm. Then suddenly when the yacht was passing through the narrow fjord just in front of Arthur, the ship went aground. Arthur had earlier moved some stakes to more shallow water. The captain shouted if he could get some help.

"Well," Arthur said, moving his pipe to the other side of his mouth, "that depends."

"How much?"

"A hundred kroner" – a huge sum in those days (1946). Arthur managed to get the yacht off the ground. The sum was paid. Everybody was satisfied. Arthur had a device for such situations which, funnily enough, occurred when he was particularly short of money. We also offered our young man in Al Askara money, but he declined. The pleasure of helping us was enough for him. Arthur was a better businessman.

We were driving farther on and camped in the dunes near the beach. We slept on our camp beds. That usually goes well, but not this night. It started to rain – not much, just a little fine rain. It was rather warm. It had been an unusual winter. A little rain now and then. Old men have never experienced that before. Usually rain comes to these parts of the country every four years, and then only a little. Early next morning the sun was shining again, and everything dried quickly. We had a swim and examined the area around us.

Big turtles crawl up to the beach from the sea in order to lay eggs in the sand during the night. We found one dead in the morning. She did not make it back to the lifesaving sea before sunrise.

We drove southwards on a gravel road – or rather a gravel track. We were heading for Masira Island where the British and the Americans have a big air base, but we are not allowed to talk about this. But we knew this base was picked out to become the headquarters during the Gulf War in case Saddam Hussein could not be stopped before he took the northern part of Saudi Arabia, including the city of Dahran. We wanted to see the beautiful nature of the island and the rich fauna.

Suddenly Bengt and Ulla had a puncture. We changed the wheel and turned back. It is not a good idea to continue without a spare tire. We should have taken two tires per car at departure, but we were careless.

When it was almost five p.m., tea time in England for vicars and old ladies, and drinks time for men, Nick stopped and came to our car, saying, "I am dangerously close to a gin and tonic." He has a facility with words, as our former boss in London said many years ago. That is true. We had our G&T.

We drove again towards the sea and stopped on top of some dunes. Then it started – a tropical storm with unbelievably heavy rain. In half an hour there was water all over. We could no longer see our track, but could identify is location from some sticks meant for such situations. Sand became mud. We decided to try to get away. We departed and were stuck again and again. We drove half an hour in water. It was fun, not dangerous – that came later. Slowly we went upwards. It was still raining. We had to assist a Bedouin who was alone in his Toyota pickup, stuck in the mud and unable to drive. It is natural to help each other when nature goes berserk. Like on the sea. We got him off. The Bedouin kissed our hands and we proceeded after the good deed. We managed to cross a couple of wadis with streaming water. It went well, but I did not like it. Sometimes the car was floating for a short moment. That was dangerous.

Nick thought we might sleep during the night in a guest house not far away. If Allah had noticed that we had helped the Bedouin he would, we thought, help us find one or two rooms in the hostel. But no, Allah had not seen us – or he had decided we should witness the enormous power of nature to teach us to be humble. Everything was full in the hostel. We had to drive on.

We did so in complete darkness. Increasing rain. We had heard that wadis can fill with water very quickly when it is raining in the mountains. Tonight there was rain overall in the Sultanate. Unusual. We thought it did not rain here. We did not believe Nick when he said that every year around seven hundred people die from drowning on the Arab peninsula, significantly more than in Europe. When it is raining here it is dangerous. Bridges and roads are swept away.

One wadi was wide, around three hundred meters. Plenty of water, trees, and rolling boulders. It was dark. We managed to get across in our big cars. Small cars were swept away when they tried to cross. After having crossed fourteen of this type of wadi, we relaxed. We could manage anything. Once again we were not right – we could not manage anything. We were stopped by a police officer who was alone with his walkie-talkie. Nick and the police officer chatted in Arabic. Yes, it was true. More water was coming down from the mountains. He advised us to turn back. Soon there would be water where we were waiting in our car. We were the first car in a long queue, but we did as demanded.

Half an hour later there was water, 1.5 meters high where we had been standing. We could now see it was dangerous. Over a wide area water was streaming. Boulders with a diameter of more than one meter were moving fast in front of us. The water would be stopped farther down where there was a dam. Water must be preserved for drier days. The level of water in front of the dam rose by ten meters that night. Just before our arrival a car with five persons had vanished in the dark. Our daughter was scared for the first time.

Many Arabs took part in the entertainment. They thought it was fun. They did not have to risk their lives crossing. Some youngsters tried to persuade drivers of motorcars to attempt a crossing, although the police officer would not allow such stupidity. One tried and made it. Another one, in a small sedan, did not. It was not heavy enough. After floating it was miraculously stopped by some sticks. The young driver survived, but the car did not. Thirteen people drowned that night. We praised Nick as a skilful leader and thanked him. He just said, "It is crisis management."

The sun was back the next day. Suddenly there were flowers all over. The children played in ponds, the leftovers from the day before.

Chapter 5

*In which one meets spring in a new way,
becomes interested in the capital, and visits
the southern part of the country.*

Spring

One can say about Oman what Rudyard Kipling said about India: "Now India is a place beyond all others where one must not take things too seriously – the midday sun always excepted. Too much work and too much energy kill a man just as effectively as too much assorted vice or too much drink."

It is now end of April. The temperature is thirty-eight degrees Celsius in the morning and forty-three in the afternoon. It is humid and difficult to go to work. One moves slowly. One does not work too hard. You stay indoors longing for the cool season, where temperatures approach twenty degrees. The wild oleanders in the wadis have blossomed for some time. The hibiscus and other spring flowers are in full bloom. The air is heavy with the scent of flowers. Good that one does not suffer from allergies. We miss Europe, where according to newspapers it is becoming warmer (i.e., around ten degrees). Our wish to go to the local swimming pool is declining. It is not cooled. But temperatures are going to be worse here in May and June. Then it is advisable to go somewhere south of Alashkara, where there is a breeze from the sea, lowering the temperature by ten degrees. People go for weekends in the mountains, like in Malaysia. Cool mountain air. It is said that Muscat is the hottest capital in the world. It is probably true for the summer season. One should not be here during late spring or summer. Everybody prefers to be inside, in the air conditioned house or in the air conditioned car. Sunroofs in cars are not seen here. The trick is to keep the sun out. The children only come out after sunset.

When I shave in the morning, I usually open the window in order to watch the beautiful brilliant yellow mountains during sunrise. It is a bit difficult to get used to the fact that the air coming through the window is not cool as at home but warm, reminding me of the air in a sauna. The roses are blossoming in the mountains. They are cultivated for production of the famous Omani rosewater, which is so popular here and abroad. The scent is a marvel, made with an ancient method of distillation, which is said to be better than modern distillation methods.

It is soon Haj, the month where Muslims travel to Mecca, or *Macca*, as they say here. There is no time to be ill. It is also becoming too hot to go to the hospital. We feel it already. Very few of the patients arrive at their scheduled time. It is not easy to know whether they will turn up some other day.

Activities in the villages are reduced. You cannot do anything in the midday heat if you have no air conditioning. Not everybody can afford it. A long rest (sleep) at noon is common, making you fresh for the evening. By mistake I entered an Omani building at noon, believing it was an official office. It was an assembly of Omani men sleeping and snoring in a room with a very high temperature, so high I almost fainted. No women were seen. They probably were preparing evening meals for the men.

The other day we visited a wadi with streaming cold, clear water from the mountains. An Omani family was sitting under a large canvas sunroof. A young man of around thirty was eating for a very long time. He was excessively fat, could hardly move, and was sweating profusely. He had to be cooled down repeatedly in the streaming mountain water. Then he could eat a little again. He will die young.

An English colleague said somewhat impolitely about Omani men, "There are only two things that interest Omani men: food and women." That is not quite true. They are also interested in cars, preferably big ones with stripes and exotic colours.

The Indians cope better with the hot climate than we do. They are used to the heat, but are not outside during the midday hours. Heat strokes are seen occasionally. I have only seen one. The case I know of from Oman was a Pakistani farm worker, who worked in the field at noon. He was saved by our hospital doctors, although with difficulty. Later he was returned to Pakistan to have psychiatric treatment. He was considered mad since he had worked in the midday sun. As in Saudi Arabia, it is important to drink often. You do not normally eat much in the heat, and you often lose weight during summer.

Then April ended, and it is now 1 May (or here 1 Dhul-Hajja 1415 AH). Now Muslims from all places on Earth are travelling to Saudi Arabia doing Haj, the yearly pilgrimage. Each country has the right to send a thousand pilgrims per million inhabitants. Elderly people have priority. The Haj culminates when the believers dressed in white climb Mount Arafat, where the Prophet preached the last time shortly before he died in the year 632. Non-Muslims (infidels) have no admittance to Mecca and Medina. However, the Western world has arrived: there is now a Burger King in Mecca.

In Copenhagen, Denmark, the students demonstrate against social injustice. In Lund, Sweden, the students are celebrating. The vice chancellor of the University of Lund speaks to them. Thus, different countries, although closely connected, have different traditions.

Muscat

Muscat is the capital. Here the Sultan has a small colourful palace with a lawn stretching to the sea, surrounded by beautiful white government buildings. The palace is mainly used for official purposes. His Majesty normally lives in his palace further north, not far from Barka. The area is discretely protected by armed soldiers. There are a couple of forts nearby.

From there everything is carefully watched. His Majesty's yacht, normally anchored in Muttrah Harbour, can anchor here so the Sultan and his guests can board from here. The yacht is bigger than *Britannia,* the former yacht of Queen Elisabeth, who could not afford to keep it. Big yachts are expensive to run. The Sultan's yacht is perhaps used once a year for foreign visits.

The British embassy was until recently neighbour to the palace in Muscat. Now the court (the Divan) has moved in. The building, one of the oldest in Oman, has a breathtaking sea view. The British embassy moved farther north, to Qurum, where the other embassies are situated and where the view is also good. There is always a breeze from the sea. Denmark has only a consulate in the business quarter of Ruwi, in an ordinary two-room flat. Business is looked after by a vice consul. Danes are modest and come from a small country. Our brothers, the Swedes have a considerably bigger consulate and they have a consul general. That sounds impressive. My uncle, who came to Denmark after World War II after having lived in South America for twenty years, thought so too. So when he was offered to become consul for Peru in Denmark, he politely refused, whereupon he was appointed consul general.

On 8 December 1764, a small English warship sailed with the monsoon from Bombay heading for Oman. Onboard was the only surviving member of the expedition of His Danish Majesty, the king of Denmark, originally sent out to explore Arabia Felix. His name was Carsten Niebuhr. After sixteen days they were near the natural harbour of Muscat. There was a storm and it was feared that the ship would be smashed to smithereens on the rocky coast. But after hard work the ship was saved. When in the harbour the first thing Carsten Niebuhr saw was a dhow loaded with figs. Its crew consisted of a number of French mercenaries, serving the Imam Ahmed bin Said, a forefather of the present Sultan. They were here after the French had lost a war with the English.

The dhow looked as dhows look today. A dhow is of old design. Its stern looks like sailing vessels from Europe in the fifteenth and sixteenth centuries: very high stern. They have a triangular sail on a special rig enabling it to sail close to the wind. The dhows are only manufactured here in Oman, in the city of Sur using ancient handicraft methods. We once encountered one at sea far away from Muscat. That was the yacht of the Finance Minister. There is something special about finance ministers with money. His son came to our boat on a water scooter. A beautiful young American girl, who was having the winter holiday of her life, sat on the backseat.

The houses at the cornice were the same as today, built by the Portuguese. That and more can be read in Niebuhr's own report, recently reprinted in 2004, and in the Danish author Thorkild Hansen's book *Arabia Felix: The Danish expedition of 1761–67* (1964). The cornice is and was very beautiful with a fantastic harbour view. Walking there during the blue hour, watching the sunset behind the mountains is unforgettable. For the time being there are two big cargo ships in the harbour, some dhows, the Sultan's huge yacht, and two Danish fishing vessels, which are slowly decaying in the suffocating summer heat.

It was a dhow which was used by Sinbad the Sailor in olden days, a copy of which was made a couple of years ago. It can now be seen on a roundabout near Al Bustan Palace Hotel. Omani seamen sailed on this ship to China. Somebody doubted this would be possible. The Omanis thus came to China before the Europeans. The Omanis have always been skilled sailors. It was an Omani man who, as a pilot, helped Vasco da Gama find his way to China. That meant the Portuguese came to dominate the trade in the Far East, and that the coastal area of Oman came under the influence of Portugal for 150 years, although Oman never became a Portuguese colony.

On the land side of the Cornice is a number of low-rise old white houses. The most beautiful ones are built by the Portuguese. Here is the entrance to the *souk*, where you can buy anything from silk, spices, frankincense, and Indian junk to gold and silver jewellery. The female members of my family have bought some Omani silver, mostly necklaces, bracelets, anklets and rings specially designed for each finger, earrings, head pieces, belts, and pendants. These items are made as they were during the time of Jesus. They are beautiful, although the handicraft is not as good as in Yemen.

You pay according to weight; handicraft is not paid for. Good books have been written on Omani and Saudi jewellery, which is increasingly hard to find. The reason is that for many years ago, a woman who inherited her mother's jewellery melted her things and had new jewellery made by the local silversmith. Later, the Bedouin women here, as in Saudi Arabia, began to sell their old silver treasures in order to be able to purchase gold jewellery, which is now becoming fashionable in Arab countries, where gold is inexpensive compared to Europe. Now the Omani women do not have so many silver items to sell, and the prices are rising. We have noticed that presently only the women in rural areas are wearing silver, while in the cities it is gold.

We buy our Omani antiques from Mohammed, who receives us as long-expected guests. Tea with sugar – only for us, not the tourists. We spend more than one hour talking with Mohammed. He appreciates that. He is presently teaching his wife selected passages from the Holy Koran. Teaching takes time. The tourists must wait. Sometimes they become impatient and leave. Mohammed does not care.

We are quite good buyers. Today we are bargaining. We did not do so earlier. I am sure Mohammed never loses money when selling something, although he does look sad when we buy a piece. It is nice that Arabs never cheat. It is against the Koran.

Mohammed is a handsome, tall, worthy man with a white beard. How old? Difficult to know. Perhaps he does not know himself. Originally he comes from Baluchistan. He speaks eight languages. He has many sons and daughters. They are all doing well being extremely polite and friendly to strangers, as is common here. The sons help their father, so they one day can take over. Unfortunately for us, prices are surging after the arrival of tourists. We now buy pottery and ceramics. Old beautiful jars can still be found at a low cost. I have it like Oscar Wilde, who said, "I can resist anything but temptation."

Our latest bargain was a colourful felt rug of a type which is only made in a remote wadi. Those rugs are difficult to find, and are very beautiful.

We tried ours this winter in the desert. Nice and warm. Now we know the soukh well, and do not go so often. Perhaps I shall go back one day in order to find an old Winchester rifle.

When I said good-bye to Mohammed, he placed his right hand over his heart, smiled, bowed his head slightly, and wished us well.

Al Bustan Palace

South of Muscat is the best hotel in Oman, Al Bustan Palace Hotel, this year as in earlier years elected by travel journalists as the best hotel in the Middle East and Africa. That is justified. The hotel is a marvel. Its origin goes back some years. The Sultan was about to host a meeting for the heads of state of the Gulf countries. He did not have proper lodging for them. The he took out his big purse and said to his people, "I want a hotel in Al Bustan."

There was a slight problem. There was already a village there. That, however, turned out not to be a problem. The houses were removed from the face of the Earth. New houses – spacious luxury villas with air conditioning – were built five hundred meters near or virtually on the beach. The villagers were fishermen. The Sultan let the fishermen know the new hotel would offer to purchase everything they could catch now and in the future. The fishermen did not protest. They got better and bigger houses and now knew they could sell the catch of the day, every day.

Then it started. In record time the hotel was finished: and featured spacious Western and Arab rooms with sea or mountain views; the biggest, tallest hall in the world; a beautiful reception area; luxury suites high up; first-class restaurants; fitness centres; and cooled swimming pools, one of them stretching from the building to the beach.

When everything was finished, it was time for a royal visit. His Majesty arrived with his entourage. Nice turbans, all with *kunjars*. It was an important day. The chief architect came creeping with his head down after the delegation. They were all in the hall. His Majesty looked discontent. "When I accepted the plans two years ago, there was a door here," he said, pointing to a wall without a door.

The chief architect blushed, fumbling with his drawings. His Majesty was right. There was meant to be a door there. But there was not. The next day there was one. His Majesty has a photographic memory. If he once has seen a face, he never forgets it. If the Sultan had not been Sultan, he would have made a good police officer.

The Airport

North of Muscat is, apart from the university, the international airport in Seeb. The Sultan has his own arrival hall and departure hall. No admittance for us commoners. He has planes of his own, big ones and small ones. His Majesty ought not to be without air transportation when needed. In our international airport for non-royal passengers there is a new tax-free shop, a curious term in a country without taxes. You can *mirabile dictu* purchase alcoholic beverages here. All arrivals and departures are announced loudly in Arabic and English. The biggest problem in Muscat Airport has always been the waiting time due to the slow procedures of passport control and changing of our money to Omani rials (RO), a change which is not possible in the European cities that I know.

The air traffic in and out of Muscat Airport is rapidly increasing. The number of passengers in the first quarter of 2014 was 2.2 million, a rise of 8.1 per cent when compared with the first quarter of 2013. Tourism is rapidly expanding and contributes significantly to the wealth of the country. A total of 37,000 people now work in the tourist sector of Oman (3.3 per cent of those employed in the country). The Omani tourist sector is the most rapidly growing sector in the Middle East. The number of tourists visiting Oman 2013 was 614,000, and in four-star or five-star hotels, 198,383, mostly from Europe, America, and the GCC (Gulf Cooperation Council) countries.

Shopping

There are small shops for "foodstuffs," etc. along the roads parallel to the motorways, but the Westerners mostly do their shopping in the modern shopping centres of the capital area. They are extremely good and for certain items cheaper than in Europe. I lost my glasses in a wadi and needed new ones. My German optician sold me some very good ones very inexpensively after having carefully tested my eyesight. This was twenty years ago, and I still have them. There are excellent shops for electronics and household devices, carpets and perfumes, and other things women like. Everything is paid in cash, even motorcars, which are extremely inexpensive here.

The Dhofar Region

The southern province of Dhofar, with boundaries to Yemen, is green and fertile, with temperatures around ten degrees lower than the rest of the country. During summer it becomes particularly green, and then it would be nice to come back. The Dhofar region is rather empty, deserted, although there are people here, particularly in the big city of Salalah. There are few but good roads. My wife found out we could fly down from Muscat inexpensively after having swapped a first-class ticket for three tourist-class tickets and three days at the Holiday Inn Hotel in Salalah.

We could have chosen to drive our own car but considered that to be too dangerous. One thousand kilometres on a boring straight road, where drivers often fall asleep, causing deadly accidents. One of our technologists had lost her husband this way. Next time we have a first-class ticket, we shall convert it to three economy tickets to Sana'a, the capital of Yemen, my wife says. But we do not. It is too dangerous there for Westerners.

We knew little of Salalah when we arrived. Now we know more. Salalah was a prosperous city in the thirteenth century due to the frankincense trade. The city later decayed, although it was the capital of Oman until Sultan Qaboos took over in 1970. Now Salalah is on the move again. The new APM terminal of Salalah was built and is managed by the Danish AP Moeller-Maersk Group, making the port of Salalah the largest of the Arab Peninsula. Salalah now has a College of Technology, and the Salalah College of Applied Science. They also have a private university. It is said that it is partly owned by a member of the Royal Family.

It is now Eid al-Adha. The Sultan says his prayers in Seeb, but we shall not witness that because we are now in Salalah, transported to this southern capital of the Dhofar region in a brand new Omani airplane. We have hired an old Toyota Land Cruiser with a double petrol tank, which can help us travel twelve hundred kilometres. There are no filling stations where we are going. We drive south-west on a good road through an extremely beautiful landscape with tall mountains. On the way we see something we had never seen before, so-called "blow holes," holes in an overhanging rock through which splashes of sea water come from the sea below. They look like the geysers in Iceland. It is peaceful here. People are either in Mecca or preparing for the big Eid al-Adha feast.

We drove until we were thirty kilometres from the Yemen/Oman border, and then we were stopped by the military. Only people with visas were allowed to proceed. Visas are difficult to get after the Gulf War, where Yemen bet on the wrong horse, Iraq. We turned left on a small road marked on our map. Its surface consisted of sharp stones. Luckily we did not have a puncture. We were in two cars for safety reasons. In the other car were Peter the pathologist and his wife, who were looking for adventure like us.

After twenty-five kilometres we reached the coast. We sighted birds we had never seen before, and trees and bushes with strange flowers. There was a steep slope, one hundred meters down to the beautiful turquoise sea. The coast south of Napoli is beautiful, but not as beautiful as this one. Here tourists will come in fifty years when there shall be luxury hotels. The present way of rural life will disappear, and the people will change.

Most of those we met had never seen Westerners before. A visiting young man had, I believe. He spoke a little English, a fact that impressed his family. We exchanged presents, things to eat and drink. There was a modern house. Our wives were invited to come inside. There sat a beautiful woman breastfeeding. She was around thirty years old and had ten children. We talked to the man, the father. The house next door also belonged to the man. Here lived his other family: another beautiful woman and another ten children. Amazing. It must be expensive. How he managed I don't know. Everybody looked happy and healthy.

I showed my Russian military binoculars to the children and the father. They had never seen such a thing before. They watched everything, saw things they could not see with the naked eye. I regret to this day that I did not give it to them. We departed with ten litres of fresh camel milk. They got our fruit. We were back before dark. Hundreds of camels were walking slowly on the road. We waited patiently.

A Danish couple is employed by the College of Science and are internationally known bird photographers. They explained to us that although many migrating birds pass over the gravel plain separating the Dhofar region from the capital area, the non-migrating birds cannot manage that distance (a thousand kilometres). Therefore the birds of the Dhofar region are different from those on Batinah Coast, where we live. Now we understand why the birds looked so African. We are closer to Africa here.

Back in Salalah everybody dressed up and celebrated the holy days. Women and girls wore velvet dresses. My wife acquired one. Now she looks very much like the natives here, also because she wears her Dhofari jewellery with pink corals.

We celebrated Eid by eating the most tender beef the world has seen. The day before we had visited the famous village of Mirbat, a big city in olden times, where we witnessed collective slaughtering of many cows. Pieces of meat were distributed in equal portions among the villagers. Pure communism.

The last day we were lying at the pool relaxing. There was Egyptian music plus something that resembled belly dancing, though it was not. Three talented Polish musicians were performing. A fat Saudi man sat with one of his fat wives drinking beer, something he is not allowed to do at home. Perhaps that is the reason he is here.

We made a small excursion to the tomb of the Prophet Job, whom we know from the Bible. He lived here in days long gone. The queen of Sheba likewise. We visited her summer residence, Samhuram, which was now a heap of ruins, but did not make it to the newly found prehistoric village of Umar. This ancient place was identified by inspecting traces of ancient tracks from the air.

But we understood why both cities (villages) came into existence: the frankincense trees, the hardened resin of which is used for manufacturing incense. The best and most expensive frankincense comes from this place, and so it was also in earlier days. As is well known the Queen of Sheba travelled to King Solomon. With her she brought frankincense as a present. The frankincense trade later made King Solomon excessively rich. The ancient Egyptians, Greeks, and Romans used it. The Omani seafarers sailed to China with it a thousand years ago. Last but not least it was and still is used by the Catholic Church. Now frankincense is used in the perfume industry. The latest news: it has been proven scientifically that it is effective against rheumatoid arthritis.

Purchasing frankincense in the soukh is a serious matter. It can take hours. There are so many varieties. We cannot smell the difference, but the Arabs can. Perhaps they cannot distinguish a good claret from a bad one. One must practice.

It was a nice holiday. I had planned to stay in Muscat to paint (I am an amateur artist), but my wife decided we should get away. I am a fool. "Take my word for it, the silliest woman can manage a clever man, but it needs a clever women to manage a fool" (Rudyard Kipling).

Chapter 6

In which one is discussing education in Oman

The Sultan Qaboos University

HM Sultan Qaboos is a clever man. He knows it is important to educate his citizens so the country does not slip back to the dark ages, when there shall be no more oil and gas, perhaps in fewer than thirty years. More than half the population is younger than fifteen. They must be educated, and they are thanks to His Majesty. It all happens here in Oman. Only specialist training takes place abroad, mostly in Europe and the Americas. Omanisation is important and takes place at an increasing rate.

The Sultan decided some years ago that he would like to have a university of his own.

His Majesty is very anglophilic. British architects were hired. The university was built in record time, and it is very beautiful: white low-rise buildings, the different colleges being spread over a large area. The surroundings are one big lush garden with many bushes and trees, and water respecting Arab garden tradition, such as streaming water in cross forms, and small waterfalls and fountains. There is a university Mosque and an impressive clock tower with bells sounding like Big Ben of London. You cannot tell the difference. There is a botanical garden, sports arenas, swimming pools, restaurants, and shops. One can live here during one's whole life without having to leave. We are here together, students and teachers. The police are looking after us. We are safe here, safer than in other places on the globe.

Omani students study eagerly. They become engineers, economists, biologists, and now also physicians. Whether they become good doctors I do not know, but those who are permitted to commence to study medicine have the highest marks in school. They will not be asked what they would like to study. They do what they are told. After having been teaching for two semesters, I must say they are very agreeable people and eager to learn. There is a general problem, in that the students here have difficulties with solutions of new problems presented to them, something they cannot read about in books. They are used to learning by heart, like they learned the Holy Koran. But physiology cannot be studied like the Koran. In physiology, you have to be able to use what you have learned in order to solve the problems presented to you, be it a patient-related problem or calculations of some complexity. Some do not possess the ability to use what they have learned at an earlier stage. Some do not have much imagination. But on the whole, they want to learn, and we do see some cases of unusual progress. You discuss everything with your professor, so one can say teaching is more individual here than in Northern Europe, which I know.

The first doctors graduated last year. A national day of celebration. His Majesty was present. This year there is also a festive atmosphere. Unfortunately, we Western teachers did not understand much of what the speakers said in Arabic. Too bad. We should study more. We are recruited to teach in a foreign country and do not learn their language properly, because everybody speaks English so well. The Sultan's Highlanders played their bagpipes. It was like being at the Edinburgh tattoo. And then the Sultan's brass band played. His Majesty has everything. Nice uniforms. Good music.

The University Hospital has its own administration run by Omanis and Filipinos. The latter are the best. However, the Omanis are friendly and eager to help. When you enter an office of an Omani, he at once puts down his newspaper. At the beginning I was rather upset by the tempo in this part of the hospital. After having worked for more than a month, I pulled myself together. I was seen creeping humbly along the walls approaching the office which was in charge of salaries to senior consultants. The young Omani put down his newspaper as expected, smiled, and asked politely what he could do for me. I asked cautiously and politely about my salary which I had not received in time. Could I perhaps have some money? The very friendly Omani man politely responded, smiling. Perhaps I could come back next week? Then perhaps there might be some money for me, *Ens'allah*, God willing. That he could do something to advance the process did not occur to him.

It is sometimes difficult to be accepted here as a fully qualified medical doctor. What is written in your application is not always believed. That is understandable when you hear that they have had applicants presenting papers from nonexistent universities. In the USA you can purchase a PhD title for 100 US dollars. The other day I noticed an advertisement in a newspaper from the Emirates with prices of a variety of academic titles. Address: a post office box in Copenhagen.

Shortly after my arrival I was summoned to an Omani female clerk. She looked reproachfully at me. I had not written the address of my school from 1943 to 1947 on my application. I corrected that with many excuses. An American doctor had a more serious problem. His school did not exist anymore. It had been removed from the face of the earth, demolished. He could not remember the address. I do not know if he was sent home.

This more or less hidden threat of being sent home reminded me of 1955, when I had got a summer job in Leverkusen, Germany. A former German military doctor asked all the applicants of the day to go into a giant room where we all were supposed to pass urine for examination before we could start working. I was not used to urinating under military command. I could not. So I was in danger of being returned to Denmark due to lack of ability to urinate. So I was told. Luckily I was able to speak German fluently in those days, and was good at scolding, storming, and raging in German. I did, and the former military doctor stood to attention and let me through. Perhaps it helped that I told him I knew his boss. Shouting is no good here in Oman. Here it is better to be diplomatic.

I was given permission to start working at the Sultan's university although not all of my papers were legalized by the Danish Foreign Ministry. I had offered to travel back to Denmark to have it done, all expenses paid, but suddenly it was not necessary to prove that I had in fact gone to school from 1943 to 1947.

One of the problems regarding the organization of the university was that girls and boys should be kept separate. That was not easy. They did go to the same lectures, but the young men sat to the left, the young women to the right. We also had such a division between sexes in our churches until recently. An Omani girl was not to be seen walking side by side with a boy. Boys and girls were not allowed to speak to each other. How to solve that problem? Very simply by building the university in two stories, so the females are kept on the top floor, the boys on the ground floor. Only old, non-dangerous university teachers like me were allowed to walk in the corridors on the first floor.

One day a male student was too close to a female student – in his car. A police car passed by. The boy's car was moving rhythmically. Oh, horror. It was not two homosexual boys, but a girl with a boy. Disaster. Instant dismissal. Home to the parents in disgrace. The girl's brothers would kill her boyfriend. But the story has a happy ending. The parents of both parties spoke to each other. It was agreed that the couple should marry. They were allowed to come back to the university after a quarantine period as a married couple to resume their studies, but of course they were not allowed to live together. That had to wait until after the final exam.

One is puzzled that the girls do not speak in public. The boys have no problem here. St. Paul the apostle recommended long ago that women remain taciturn in public, and here they do. Generally the girls perform better than the boys. Apparently they are more studious. Whether they are more intelligent is another matter.

There is a dress code. For young male students it is a *disdasha* (tunic) and the Omani cap with or without a turban. For female students it is long dresses and *abaya* plus scarf, all in black. Veiling is not allowed at the university, only at home with the parents and when the lady is picked up Thursday afternoons by her brother to be driven home to the village.

Everything is in English. This is a British university in the Middle East. The first two years after your A-levels you have to study English in order to become fluent in spoken and written English. Then you can be admitted. Not one textbook is in Arabic, because the Sultan has decided he wants a British university. So all textbooks are in English. Imagine that our youngsters at home were obliged to study Arabic before they were allowed to begin at the university, and then only use books in Arabic.

We often have visitors from abroad, delegations of politicians and administrators at a high level. I have entertained the former prime minister of Jordan, who incidentally is a medical doctor. Those who have been here longer have talked to other top politicians like President Francois Mitterrand of France and Prime Minister Margaret Thatcher of Great Britain. The latter was perhaps here because her son's company had won the contract to build the university. Funny coincidence. Professor SE Lindell of Sweden was one of the founders of the university and was photographed while talking to the Sultan at a recent royal visit.

The Omanis are proud of our department, the department of clinical physiology, the only one in the Middle East, because we have a lot of modern diagnostic equipment. For example, we have the only whole-body counter in the Middle East. It can measure radioactive contamination in persons, something that became important after Chernobyl. It can also be used for physiological studies, and we do perform such studies.

I am now a senior consultant in Oman. There is no guarantee for a lifelong occupation once you are in. You get a contract for two years. If you do not live up to expectations, your contract will not be renewed – or if money has to be saved, even those who have been here many years risk dismissal, because they are more expensive than the new arrivals. Grounds for dismissal are not given. However, the top administrators understand the value of experience. It is not unknown in this part of the world that old people are cleverer than young people because they have experience.

This spring a number of university teachers were nervous. One day some received the much-feared brown envelope. That means farewell to Oman and to a monthly salary. Not that the salary is impressive, although one makes thirty times more than the Indian gardener looking after your plants and flowers, or the man who washes your car at the filling station. However, it is rather awful for a middle-aged university teacher to lose his or her job without having anything to come back to. When you come back to your country you will not be able to afford to have a gardener, a cleaning lady/ man and a lady for washing and ironing your shirts.

The university has no official age for retirement, one is not safe when older than sixty. The internationally recognized ornithologist Professor Fry is approaching sixty, and this year he got the brown envelope. He was expecting it. Now he will have more time to finalize ongoing work (such as the last two volumes of his great work, *Birds of Africa*). It is not nice to know that one is not needed anymore; like Winston Churchill after the war, when the English voters rejected him in spite of all he had done for Britain and the free world. His wife, Clementine, tried to comfort him by saying, "This might be a blessing in disguise," to which Winston Churchill replied, "If so, it is well disguised." Later he enjoyed his temporary retirement by painting in North Italy.

The other day I reminded the hospital director, Nasser, that he was sixty-three. "Shh," he said, "nobody knows."

Here people often do not know their exact age, because the time of your birth was not written down in earlier times. One should in fact celebrate the time of conception, because that would be justified thinking of those who were born prematurely.

Nasser has a sense of humour. One day I was waiting for him in front of his office. I had a problem I wanted to discuss. Several others also wanted a chat with him. An English head nurse passed by. When she saw the crowd waiting and Nasser approaching, she waved to him, saying, "Nasser, I do not need your services anymore."

He turned around and said with a smile, "What a terrible thing for woman to say to a man."

Every Wednesday afternoon the spacious lecture hall is filled with students and doctors. Experienced lecturers and young Omani doctors present difficult cases, which are subsequently discussed. Good exercise. The British academics are good teachers. There are lectures and seminars. Excellent. Worth listening to.

International Congresses

Sometimes international congresses are organized in Oman. Once I helped organize an orthopaedic congress for the Gulf countries at the Al Bustan Palace Hotel. Interesting experience with surprises. I had a couple of short presentations with low attendance. Then I was co-chairman at a session in the main lecture hall, which was full. Nobody had asked me, if I would accept, but it was written in the program. It was a session on war surgery, a subject I knew nothing about. Luckily I was there, because my co-chairman never turned up. After the papers I had allotted time for discussion.

An American orthopaedic surgeon showed statistics from his army hospital during the Gulf War. A Saudi doctor had been head of department at another hospital nearby. The Saudi doctor accused the American colleague of lying. The Saudi doctor had only operated on forty minor injuries, and the American doctor told us about four thousand serious injuries on Iraqis and Saudi soldiers. At his hospital a number of soldiers from the West were made transportable so they could be evacuated to Frankfurt for final treatment. No doubt this war had been more serious than the public and the Saudi doctor believed. The American surgeon showed photos of war injuries (children without hands, which had been blown away when they picked up what they believed to be toys or cigarette packets).

It was an interesting war, the Gulf War, when you sat at home watching TV, looking at the precision bombings carried out by the Americans.

Damages were not insignificant. Nick says the same. He was in Riyadh. The houses had no basements so he stood on his terrace watching the events. He showed me a unique photo: a scud missile being shot down by an American missile before reaching the centre of Riyadh.

My colleague Graham was chairman too. He had a Saudi co-chairman. He had arrived in time. Graham reminded his co-chairman that the speakers should keep the time.

He would make sure they did, the Saudi said. When the first speaker had used half his time, the Saudi chairman demonstrated his newly acquired power by saying, "Stop, sit down. I do not agree with you."

The poor man then sat without having had a chance to say what he had travelled hundreds of kilometres to say. The Saudi co-chairman looked as if he was pleased with himself and his toughness.

Academic discussions at congresses in this part of the world are rare. I once was threatened to be killed when I tried to discuss a diagnosis with a Syrian doctor. He apparently felt that I had hurt him seriously. After that time I try to be very gentle. When I criticize colleagues from the Middle East, I even sometimes tell them how marvellous they are. Or I say nothing. That is easier. A discussion here of a doctoral thesis would be impossible. The academic discussion takes time to develop.

It reminded me of my first time in Rio de Janeiro. A young Japanese doctor spoke on the bone density values of one thousand Japanese women, an impressive number, never done before. I forgot to praise him. Conversely, I told him he had wasted his time, that his material in its present form was useless because he did not correct for age (bone density declines with age). He looked as if he could have killed me. In fact he probably would rather kill himself (hara-kiri), especially when his professor, who had travelled with his promising young doctor, now loudly told the young man he was a fool. And he was. I should not have said anything, but it was warm and the audience needed to be cheered up.

The Campus

Recently we said good-bye to a dear friend and colleague, Sven-Eric, who with Nasser founded the medical school here. There was a mini-symposium. Nasser made a little speech about the co-operation they had had, a very successful one. Initially they travelled a lot in order to recruit staff for the new hospital. They also came to Copenhagen. Sven-Eric invited Nasser to the Royal Opera House of Copenhagen. Nasser had no feeling for that kind of music, which honestly is quite different from Arab music. He fell asleep snoring loudly. After the opera he woke up and said, "Thank you, Sven-Eric, I enjoyed that," to which Sven-Eric replied: "What did you enjoy, the opera or the sleep?"

I must not forget the libraries, those holy places of knowledge and wisdom. The libraries are often rather full because the air conditioning here is better than elsewhere. Very smart. Apart from the medical library and the libraries of the other colleges, there is a large common library where there should be books on Oman, which I would like to study. "It was easy to get in, difficult to get out," as my psychiatric friend Knud said, when I was about to visit him in his department of psychiatry at home. People looked oddly at me. Had I done something wrong? Yes, I had by mistake entered the library for women. I hurried away, wanting to leave this dangerous place in order to come down to the library for men.

I opened a door where something was written in Arabic, which I could not read. That I should not have done. A bell or rather several bells rang loudly. I hurried back to the female library. Tried another door. Even more alarm bells. Then I was arrested. I was escorted down to be interrogated, wanted for questioning. Subsequently they released me when they found out I was not a dangerous criminal intending to attack the young ladies who had to be protected against passionate men like me. I have not been in this library since that day. It is too dangerous. I keep thinking of the Omani prisons.

Most of the foreigners employed by the university live in semi-detached houses on campus. There are different types, one for singles and married couples and one for families with children. We have one of those: three bedrooms and three bathrooms. There is no difference between academics and non-academics. The only persons receiving special treatment are the deans, who have villas with domestic wings.

HM Sultan Qaboos is busy and works long hours. Occasionally he drives on campus without his usual entourage, not in disguise like Harun al Rashid, but anonymously. He has been here again in his Land Rover Discovery. Two years ago he was also here. What is he doing? He looks at our trees, bushes, and flowers. This time he thought it was a bit barren. The next day saw an army of Indian gardeners. Now it looks fantastic, thanks to His Majesty. The trees are already growing.

Here on campus we are forty different nationalities, and we have neither racial nor language problems. Everybody speaks English with different accents. Our friend Polish Joe has a very charming accent. The other day he told me how he ended up in England.

As a child he was in Warsaw, eight years old, when the Germans invaded Poland. He stood on the balcony when it all started. He watched the shooting until his mother came home from work. They both went to the basement and stayed there for two months. The mother, being a doctor, had received a sack of flour as a fee from a patient. This was better than cash and kept them alive. They found water in some old wells.

A long time after that, when the Russians were approaching, the Germans removed the houses of Warsaw by dynamite. After that senseless total destruction of one of the nice old capitals of Europe, they withdrew to the West. After the war, his mother looked for her husband. He was also a doctor and had disappeared during the first days of the war. With great difficulty he had reached Great Britain, where he volunteered to fight as a soldier in a Polish regiment. At the end of the war he was in Italy. He succeeded in coming with a Red Cross expedition to Warsaw. There he found a local aid station the purpose of which was to reunite families split during the war. He asked a nice lady there, who said, "That is curious. I talked with your wife yesterday. She is looking for you, but was convinced you were dead." All three went to England.

In fact they were not three people but four. Joe had an adopted sister. Joe's father was distantly related to a Jewish family, caught in the Warsaw ghetto. Slowly the Jews in the Ghetto began to realize the Germans would actually kill them all, and the ten-year-old Jewish girl was smuggled out through the sewage system. She found a home with Joe's family. One week later the Ghetto was closed, all surviving Jews being sent to Auschwitz. The girl was sent to a cloister when the houses adjacent to the Ghetto were searched. There she was not found. She had forgotten her biological parents, but would have liked to have a picture of them. After she came to London, the only surviving member of her family was traced, a ninety-year-old aunt of her mother. She lived in the United States and sent her only family photo when writing to the young lady: "You and your parents are in this photo, but since I cannot see, I cannot point them out for you."

It is bad to lose one's past, but the girl is married in Holland where she lives close to her grown-up children.

It is not often you meet people who can tell you how it was in Poland during the war.

We help each other in case of problems of any kind. Recently I had a rather special problem. After having painted in the afternoon sun (the picture on the cover) I became a little dizzy. After having swallowed a litre of mineral water, I packed my gear, switched on the engine, and suddenly my car was standing on the top of a big boulder. It was 1 x 2 x 2 meters. I had not seen it, perhaps because I was dehydrated due to the heat. How I got there I do not know.

The situation was this: My car could not come down due to lack of contact between the wheels and the boulder. I climbed down, grasped my last bottle of water, and started walking the ten kilometres home. I found an Omani chap sitting in his car with his girlfriend enjoying the beautiful view in his air conditioned car. He drove me home. My friends took me back to my car in their big cars armoured with tools of different kinds. We succeeded in getting the car down without too much damage and got home to my place. I drove my own car. That evening we drank a lot of beer.

The social life here is more intense than at home in Northern Europe. We eat and drink too much, but we like it. There are farewell parties and welcome parties, parties for the newcomers so they can meet those with whom they are going to work. At home it would be expensive to have a good party. Not here, where a bottle of champagne costs one tenth the price at home.

The Children of Expatriates

Early morning is a busy time on campus. The children are going to school, or rather they are taken to school in school buses. There is a variety of schools and many buses. The schools have this in common: they are all located far away from the university. There are Filipino schools, Indian schools, and English-American schools.

The best English-American school is the British-American Academy. That is our daughter's school. She loves it. It takes half my salary every month, but it is worth it. This is a competitive school where the children learn well, not like at home where the pupils are not supposed to learn something that not all pupils can learn. That is of course bad for the academic future of a country. Here there are a hundred tests per class per year. In our Omani school, the pupils can choose between a variety of subjects. There is discipline which the pupils do not feel suffocating.

Smoking is forbidden. Last year a girl was sent away permanently because she had smoked twice in spite of one warning. She had been given cigarettes by her parents, who were both chain smokers. In Denmark we convert classrooms to smoking rooms for the pupils. In Omani schools, smoking is simply not tolerated.

The girls do not buy expensive clothing for wearing at school. That is forbidden. Here we have a dress code. With long intervals there are "mufti" days. Then the pupils may dress as they please without affronting public decency. The "mufti" days remind me of a Buddhist temple I visited in Tokyo. The monks normally were not allowed to speak, but once a month speaking was allowed. Then all the monks ran around screaming and talking loudly.

After school there are a multitude of activities. The school has several orchestras and a lot of sports activities. Our daughter was taught to sail laser dinghies at the Al Bustan Palace Hotel. Perhaps she thought of her friends at home in the dark cold climate of February, when there is probably rain, sleet, and snow but no sun.

Now it is exam time. It is too warm to be outside. Now the young pupils sit down and study. They all want good marks. Here is competition in a healthy way. Our French-Algerian colleague has two sons and one daughter. They are all doing well. Her eldest son is the best pupil in the school. He was recently accepted for MIT (Massachusetts Institute of Technology). He had correctly answered 95 per cent of the questions, something which had not been seen before. Subsequently he got the best A-levels in the history of Oman. His mother donated cakes and his uncle in Algiers sent $60,000 to the promising young man for his future studies. One might envy the Arab family bonds.

The students at the university are also studying, preparing for the exams of the year in one month. After that they will leave in order to go home to see parents and friends in their village.

Chapter 7

In which one debates the Omanis and their ruler, and discusses Omani women

The Omanis

We do not know many Omanis well. That has to do with the fact that we do not speak Arabic well. But we like them. Never before have we met so much spontaneous friendliness and helpfulness as here in Oman.

My friend Nasser, the hospital director, is a kind man. He has finalized the building of a spacious villa on the beach. Many expatriates would have liked to live there, but only Omanis are allowed to own property in Oman. Nasser does not want too many green plants in his garden. As he says, "Watering plants is too expensive, and my retirement is approaching."

Nasser's great-grandfather was buying and selling slaves; he was the richest slave dealer in German East Africa. He had received the Iron Cross from the German Kaiser. I have seen a photo of this interesting man in Nasser's villa. The family lived for many years in Zanzibar, so Nasser speaks Swahili better than Arabic. His English is perfect. He has a Filipino secretary and an Arab secretary. The latter looks after his Arab correspondence, since Nasser does not write or read Arabic well. When you cannot read what you sign, you need to have confidence in your secretary.

Satellite antennae are presently a status symbol in Oman. Nasser has two, each two meters in diameter. He can watch TV from all over the world,

China included. That he likes. Other leading Omanis whom we know also live by the sea, not on campus, where the houses are small, although spacious enough for us.

It is not often we are invited home like with Nasser. The Omanis frequently entertain in restaurants, like the French. Usually parties with Omanis take place without the wives, who stay at home. The other day we were invited to such an event. There were many Omanis. I again thought how cleverly they dress. Loose clothing, thin materials, no sweating. Barefoot or in sandals, which you take off whenever you like. We talked quietly and politely. Juice was served. We usually take a drink before and after – not because we are alcoholics, but because we are used to it.

The Omanis maintain this is their country. Here is plenty of space. The government has decided that every Omani man can have a gift from the government (the price is symbolic), namely two pieces of land. On the first one he can build a house, when his family has found him a wife, and on the second one he can build a house for his business.

Family is of paramount importance. It is important to belong to the right tribe. As in Europe, it does not hurt to have a respected family name. It is said few Omani families help the Sultan govern the country, being members of the government and having influential jobs. Some are closer to the Sultan than others. The Zanzibar Omanis are not considered as distinguished as other families, and therefore rarely reach the top of Omani society. It has perhaps something to do with the fact that their Arabic is not perfect, but they are well-educated and well-trained.

There are many Arab dialects. But a doctor from Egypt can easily speak to an Omani patient. They say the most beautiful and classical Arabic is the language spoken in Egypt. When you hear classical Arabic spoken on TV or radio, you must admit the language is beautiful, but we do not understand it. Nor can we read their script, but it looks decorative.

It is interesting that due to the rapid expansion of Islam centuries ago, people in the entire Middle East and North Africa can today talk with each other. It is not surprising that they for centuries again and again have tried to form one big Arab (Islamic) nation. It would be frighteningly strong if political unanimity could be obtained, but that seems to be difficult.

We learned recently that Urdu, the language of Pakistan, and Swahili, the language spoken in large parts of East Africa are so related to Arabic that people from those countries can lean Arabic rather easily. For us Europeans, it is difficult. Curiously enough there are certain mountainous areas of southern Oman and Yemen where they speak a pre-Arabic language, a Nilo-Hamitish dialect, which is so different from Arabic that when patients from those isolated areas come to our hospital, we can only communicate with them if that day there is a person present who comes from the district they come from. The people from those areas are tall and slim like the Ethiopians, Somalis, and Nubians.

More and more Europeans return home, and more and more Omanis are employed by the university. This is natural, but we hope the Omanis do not take over prematurely. There are certain problems with the omanisation. A Canadian colleague said, "You must employ three times as many Omanis as foreigners in order to have the same work done."

An English colleague said somewhat unkindly about the subordinate Omanis: "First come their genitals, then comes their family, and then their work." We have often had to wait for an Omani employee because his grandmamma had to be driven to the airport or his sister had her birthday. That will improve in a couple of generations, I believe.

Many Omanis have an extra job. It is easy to understand that the wish to make money is big here where no tax is paid and the salaries for people working for the Omani authorities are not high. So people often have a second job.

In my youth, we had a professor in my hospital in Denmark who did not work hard at his department. In fact, he only worked from nine to noon, three hours, although he was paid for eight.

His boss, the hospital mayor, a female social democrat, told him she expected some more work in the future, to which he replied, "Dear mayor, having paid me a moderate salary over the years, you cannot expect more from me."

He was not sacked but retired early, and thereafter lived from the income he received from the sales of a tablet he had invented and had mass produced. It was a multivitamin tablet with minerals.

A journalist had decided to interview this interesting man who, unlike most doctors, was a successful businessman, and he asked the professor, "Sir, now that you have invented this new tablet, don't you think that the tablet should undergo some kind of scientific test?"

The professor replied, "Young man, I am almost seventy years old. I really do not have the time." A self-made man. When you are badly paid, it is natural that you seek new sources of income.

Our professor of pharmacology got permission to employ an extra keeper to look after the animals for experimental pharmacology. There was only one condition: he had to be Omani.

They found one who was ready to take the job. He only stayed one day. "I want office," he said. An office was not offered. Why did the man want an office? Because when you have an office, you also have a telephone. When you have a telephone, you can do business. When you can do business, you can make money. And that was the whole idea. The man wanted to make money. The low salary of the job then became less important.

Concerning business, recently one of the professors wanted to sell his car because he was leaving. He talked to the driver employed by the College of Medicine. This man was probably the lowest paid person at the university. That did not affect him. "I shall fix that," he said. And so he did. He had a workshop in Seeb, and from there he also sold second-hand cars. In a couple of hours he had sold the car. He gave five thousand Omani rials to the professor, who was delighted. He himself got 1 per cent in provision. He makes more money than the professors.

It is a matter of discussion whether the Omanis are less efficient than we are. In many ways they are worth more than we are. For example, they can talk to the patient without an interpreter. We cannot do that. A good interview and a thorough case story are worth a lot.

We often discuss the differences between the Omanis and us. One colleague claims that the subjunctive does not exist in Arabic. I don't know, but I have noticed that our Omani patients have difficulty understanding a theoretical situation. For example, when the doctor says, "If you have stomach pain you must take two of these tablets, and then come back to the hospital," such a theoretical situation seems difficult to handle. A typical answer is, "But I have no stomach pain, doctor."

The hospitality of Arabs is well-known, and well described by Wilfred Thesiger in his book *Arabian Sands,* an interesting, often-poetic description of his journeys on camelback in Oman and the Rub' al Khali Desert, also called the Empty Quarter, because normally there are no people, only an occasional camel caravan. He was a lone wolf, came close to the Bedouins, dressed like they did, and spoke their language. He travelled with little luggage, but always had his Leica camera at hand. His books are marvellously illustrated with his black-and-white photos from the time before civilization came to the Arab peninsula twenty-five years ago. When he came back to Oman by invitation from His Majesty, he quickly left the country because he could not stand seeing the spoiled nature and the tangible signs of Western influence.

We have met the famous guest hospitality in the interior several times. During an excursion to the city of Fanja, I asked an Omani man if he could show us the best route to this small city. He was most obliging, showing us everything in detail. He invited us to visit him and his family in his new house with a beautiful view over the wadi Fanja. We spent a couple of hours with civilized conversation, said hello to some of his children, (but naturally not his wives). Our host was an elected member of the *Majlis Ash'ura*, which is consulted by the government, or used for orientation by the government when decisions have been made, and the royal decrees decided. This is a cautious beginning of democracy which, according to the Sultan's view, should be introduced slowly. The coffee was good. Real Omani coffee with cardamom and rosewater, served in small cups with a glass of cold water and accompanied by home grown dates of superior quality. Luckily we did not have lunch. I dislike watching Arabs eating rice and pieces of meat with their hand, although they only use their right hand. Perhaps I shall get used to it.

After the coffee, our host took us to the big decayed local fort, which has never been excavated or seen by archaeologists. If I were an archaeologist or a historian, I would come to Fanja and start digging. It is not common knowledge that Oman has a large number of forts, some of which are very old. The Arab forts came first, before the European forts. The crusaders learnt to build forts from the Arabs, when they met them in their efforts to conquer the "Holy Land," by some today called Palestine, by others Israel, and in Saudi Arabia termed "Enemy-Occupied Palestine." On printed maps here, the country has no name. In Saudi Arabian newspapers, the country is removed with black ink, like pictures of women.

The educated Omanis are sometimes a bit worried that the future of the country is dubious, because the oil prices are declining. The US dollar, to which the rial is connected at a fixed exchange rate, has also been falling lately in relation to the Japanese yen. Oman has solved the problems by selling more oil and gas, whereby the oil reserves are being emptied more quickly than planned, and the prices per unit are falling. At a recent meeting with the Majlis Ash'ura, the Minister for Development informed the members that new, rather large amounts of oil and gas have been found. What a relief. The authorities had begun mumbling about direct taxes, but that has stopped now. We do hope the Finance Minister will not decide to come to Scandinavia, where he could learn a lot about direct and indirect taxation. So far the authorities restrict themselves to charges on driving licenses, hotel accommodations, liquor licenses, visas, etc., which foreigners will pay, not Omani citizens. The foreigners can afford it, it seems to be believed. You get a lot of information when you talk to people who have regular meetings with ministers. Unfortunately they have introduced a tax on wages and salaries for all firms having foreigners as employees. That means our school will become more expensive, but it is good for the omanisation.

Understanding the past makes it easier to understand the present. We shall here restrict ourselves to what can be remembered by people living today or what living people have heard told by others. The surgeon Timothy Harrison, now seventy years old, is an interesting man. He grew up in an interesting family. His father, Dr Paul Harrison, was a doctor and a missionary in Oman during the 1930s, the only doctor in this country. He operated under primitive conditions without electricity or running water in his small hospital in Muscat. He wrote a book on his interesting life, *Doctor in Arabia*. He saved many, but some died. Of course it happened that patients died of complications. The reactions of family members then became threatening. It had been difficult to persuade patients and family members to allow the operation. It did not become easier when the patient died.

The experienced doctor travelled a great deal in this country on the back of a camel. Tim often accompanied his father on another camel. One day the father had had enough. He imported a motorcar with six cylinders and big wheels. Tim remembers when one day they came to a village. While his father was busy examining patients, Tim saw the villagers, after having watched the vehicle with disbelief, put a big pile of hay in front of the car. The animal should have something to live on, they apparently decided.

Tim was the only non-Arab child in Muscat at the time. He remembered everything: the camel transports and the unbearable heat in May and June. He also told us of the time he knew Sultan Qaboos's older brother. Perhaps the royal brother was sorry he did not become Sultan. It was shortly after Sultan Qaboos's takeover. The country was still very primitive. This royal person now asked Tim if he would like to see his electric light. Tim agreed. They travelled north – on camelback – to where the brother lived.

After some days they reached their destination, a small, unimpressive house with only one room. The host went inside, started the generator. "Let there be light, and there was light" (Genesis). The plaster fell down the walls. Everybody applauded. This was worth the journey. They had the first electric light in the country. In those days, at the Renaissance, there was only three kilometres of paved road without streetlights. Now, after twenty-five years, there are motorways all over – with lights.

Dr Don Bosch, also a missionary, came to this country when the present Sultan was young. Bosch told about Sultan Qaboos's father. Sultan Said was not an unintelligent man, but it was his honest conviction that it would not be good for his people to change anything at all, especially if the new things came from the United States or Europe. In those days the city gate was closed at ten p.m., as it had been the custom for hundreds of years. That was also the case in Copenhagen until a little more than a hundred years ago. The Omanis needed no education, he believed. Everything was in the Holy Koran. Men were allowed to read so much that they could read the Holy Koran. All the women in Oman naturally were illiterate. They should have children and look after things at home. It was said the old Sultan was so old fashioned he had forbidden his subjects to use glasses. The Holy Koran said nothing about this newfangled nonsense.

His Majesty Sultan Qaboos

The young Prince Qaboos graduated from the Royal Military Academy, Sandhurst. He spent one year in Germany as an officer at a British Infantry Battalion and held a staff appointment with the British army. He then embarked on a world tour and later spent six years in Oman studying the history of Oman and Islam. He could see changes were needed, and he said so. He was disobedient. His father placed him under house arrest for a couple of years. However, the young man succeeded in deposing his father through a bloodless military coup. It seemed the British were behind it. They could see that communist rebellious people in the Dhofar region supported by the communist South Yemen could not be controlled by Prince Qaboos's father. When soldiers forced their way to Sultan Said in order to arrest him, he took his revolver from the drawer of his office desk in order to defend himself – and shot himself in the foot. He was flown out of the country by the British Royal Air Force for surgical treatment in Cyprus. He lived to the end of his days at the Dorchester Hotel in London.

For some time, unrest in the Dhofar region prevailed. The new Sultan solved the problems with shrewdness, like he solved all other problems in the years to come. However, the relation to Yemen remained cool, it is said. It did not help that Yemen bet on the wrong horse during the Gulf war (Saddam Hussein). The latest news is that one can now again fly from Muscat to Sana'a, but crossing the border by car remains difficult.

HM Sultan Qaboos has converted a backward country to a modern state in twenty-five years. Earlier divisions between tribes are now reduced. The wise ruler has assembled advisers and ministers around him who were earlier adversaries. We often in the newspapers see pictures of the government taken during the yearly "Meet the People Tour." The Sultan is in the middle. Two rows of ministers, one of each side of His Majesty, are all simply dressed in turbans, disdashas (tunics), and sandals. The Sultan is unarmed, but the ministers have rifles. It would be easy for one of them to shoot his ruler.

As far as I can see in the pictures of the somewhat overweight ministers, none of them look like Cassius described in Shakespeare's play *Julius Caesar*. Julius Caesar says, "Let me have men about me that are fat; sleek headed men and such as sleep o'night; yond Cassius has a lean and hungry look; he thinks too much; such men are dangerous."

Apparently Oman is a peaceful country, but you never know. My father wrote home to Denmark from Germany the last week of August 1939: "I do not believe the rumours of a forthcoming war. Here it is peaceful, and I have not seen a single soldier." I still have the postcard. Likewise in Oman. It is so peaceful here. However, shortly after our arrival to the country we from Paris heard rumours that thousands had been arrested here in Oman. The only thing we noticed was that some students were missing. The version which is most close to the truth is probably this: The Indian secret service warned the Omani government that a rebellion was about to start. Some Indian Muslim fundamentalist circles had been uncovered and in this connection some Omani names came up. Big depots of weapons were found at different places in the country. It was more than hinted that the rebellion had been initiated abroad. Later there was unrest in Bahrain. What should one believe? The newspapers were silent. The only official reaction was that His Majesty had converted some death sentences to life in prison. Then they can sit there and contemplate. There is no air conditioning in the Omani prisons. The heads of the rebellion were said to have been executed.

The Sultan survived. When he took over in 1970 he was believed to have a 50 per cent chance of dying a natural death. He is still around. On the National Day, His Majesty made a very clever and well-phrased speech about tolerance and fighting against any form of extremism. It was quoted in the world press. Nobody let him down during the crisis described above. Everybody supported him, something very unusual in the Middle East. Even the period after a victory can be risky for the head of state. Generals can become reckless after having had success.

Here is a story about Field Marshall Bernard Montgomery. After the battle of El Alamein, Montgomery was more self-confident than ever. There was a meeting in London between Montgomery, Winston Churchill, and King George. Montgomery spoke a lot.

After he left, Churchill grunted, "Your Majesty, I think this man is after my job."

"Thank God," said the King. "I thought he was after mine."

His Majesty leads a simple life compared to other Arab leaders. The Sultan knows when money has to be saved. He cuts down the staff of the royal yacht. He does not drive big, expensive cars. He has an old Land Rover Discovery. He has been photographed while speaking to ordinary people, dressed like them. However, he carries a royal turban, only permitted for members of the Royal Family. Everybody has access to him. When he is in the countryside, far away from the royal palaces, he lives and works in a tent. Foreign heads of state must visit him there if they want to talk to him. That happened to the British Prime Minister, John Major. He wanted to sell some military hardware to Oman. He came to see the Sultan in his tent. There they sat on a rug discussing military problems.

Latest news: The first good news is that Sultan Qaboos has signed an agreement with the president of Yemen, Mr Saleh, concerning the border between the two countries. Not bad. Now the troops on both sides will withdraw from the border area. The second good news is that travel agencies in Oman can now arrange tourist trips to Amman and Petra in Jordan with a subsequent trip to east and west Jerusalem plus a tour to Bethlehem and other biblical sites. The third good news is that an Israeli ambassador will be coming to Oman soon.

His Majesty is praised everyday in newspapers, on radio, and on TV. Every book which is published here has in its preface some words of well-deserved praise. It was the same in my country, Denmark, when we had absolute monarchy. Whether the Sultan came to power by his own effort or he was pushed on to the throne by the British, he has done a marvellous job, and he has survived for twenty-five years. The Omanis are not afraid of discussing the Sultan, how proud they are, like the French are not ashamed of talking of "la Gloire de la France." Shakespeare said in *Twelfth Night*, "Be not afraid of greatness: some are born great, some achieve greatness, and some have greatness thrust upon them." About His Majesty, one can perhaps say that he is a great man, and he has become that by a combination of the three methods.

What shall happen when the Sultan is no longer here? One can only guess. He is unmarried and has no children. It is said he wants an elected president to succeed him.

Omani Women

Veiling is not uncommon in the interior, but most Omani women are not veiled. When you look at them, and it is difficult not to because they are often very beautiful. They often hide themselves behind a little bit of their veil in front of their face.

Nick claims his wife has a black belt in shopping. Mine has too. Many Omani women have one. One is tempted to believe it is normal for women to have it. Women who are shopping are often very concentrated and can be watched without them seeing you. Omani women are quality conscious. One day I was window shopping. I considered buying some gold for the female members of my family. Inside was a man with three veiled wives. They were looking at gold bracelets. They are going to have the same. According to the Holy Koran, wives must be treated identically. It is going to be expensive. Poor man. Good that we do not have polygamy in Europe. You could only see their eyes. What eyes. Beautiful, black eyes. One spotted me watching her. She winked and waved her hand. I had to go.

"Say to the believing women that they should lower their gaze and guard their modesty, that they should not display their beauty" (Koran 24.31). Preferably a woman should only show her eyes, but even the eyes can be hidden by a semi-translucent veil through which she can see but not be seen. The veil protects the woman against the oversexed looks of the men. It is not the men's fault they are so passionate. God has made them like this. Therefore women must hide their tempting bodies behind a lot of clothing, so only her husband can enjoy their beautiful body and face. That is quite simple. Women who expose themselves (naked arms, ankles, and face) are somewhat suspect and are easily considered suffering from looseness. Decent Omani women, however, scamper about with expensive perfumes (the world's most expensive perfume, Amouage, is manufactured in Oman), expensive shoes and handbags. And they paint their hands and feet with henna, something which can be very elegant. It is said they please their husbands by painting their private parts with henna.

"Every bit of hair on a woman's face is like a dagger in the heart of the martyrs of Islam," said Nick the other day. That is how they look at it in Saudi Arabia, but not here. In Saudi Arabia the *mutawas* (religious police) are beating women for showing their hair. They use big sticks, and it hurts. An English nurse had worked for some years in Riyadh. Now she had had enough and came to Oman. She arrived at the same time as us. She told us this story: A Canadian women was shopping in one of the biggest supermarkets in Riyadh. She was accompanied by her husband, a Canadian diplomat. Going shopping alone is strictly forbidden; you must be accompanied by your father, brother, or husband. She was decently dressed with long sleeves, etc., but a little bit of hair could be seen in front of her headscarf. A mutawa spotted her; he came closer and without warning began beating the wife up with his big stick. Her husband naturally protested. What happened? The mutawa pushed him so that he fell on a moving escalator and broke his neck. He was instantly dead. The mutawa walked away.

The display of hair and a women's naked skin can lead to rape. Some Muslim immigrants to Europe sometimes go berserk when they see the skin of women or even naked women on the beach, which is not uncommon in Scandinavia. They are not used to that.

In Saudi Arabia, a woman must produce three male witnesses in court if she claims to have been raped. That can be difficult. If she cannot, she may be executed. It is the woman's fault if she is raped, because she is so tempting. Wilfred Thesiger tells from the Rub' al-Khali (the empty quarter) that a young girl had been raped. She failed to produce three male witnesses. She was shot by her brother. The perpetrator was lashed, so they must have believed the girl. Why did she have to die? Because it was now impossible to find a husband for her, and she would remain a lifelong burden for the family. It is obvious that not many cases of rape are reported.

In modern Oman it is not that bad. Men and women look with disapproval on Western women who are not decently dressed. My wife and daughter are. They always wear a head scarf, and my wife never leaves home without her *abbaya*. That is appreciated. They are, however, never veiled, but perhaps they should be, because veiling protects women against the men. An American woman was visiting Oman. She dressed up like an Omani woman with veil, etc., which Westerners are not allowed to do. She later described in an America newspaper the freedom she felt. She could watch the men. They could not see her.

A British well-trained and fit military instructor drove his car to the beach with his wife. She stayed in the car while he was walking a little bit. Two Omani men approached the car and tried to open the doors. She was not covered and may have tempted the men by looking good. Her husband saw what was going on and hurried back to the car. He caught the two men, tied them up, and took them to the nearest police station. Each got six years in prison. The British instructor thought it was a bit much, but the judge said to him, "That is if they behave well; if they do not, it shall be more." That was a bit of a punishment. There is no air conditioning in Omani prisons. If they have no family, they will have no food, it is said. In Europe they could have gone home without being jailed. In Saudi Arabia they might also have been considered innocent. A non-veiled woman sitting there, tempting the passionate men. It is not their fault that they are passionate. God made man passionate. I tell this story to illustrate the fact that Omani authorities do a lot in order that Westerners can feel safe here.

One could say it is immaterial how you are dressed. But it is not. In Bahrain, there was unrest recently. It was said that this was due to the fact that the Western residents and tourists there provoked the locals with their Western way of dressing, believe it or not. But it is wise to adhere to the rules and recommendations when you live in an Arab country or visit it as a tourist.

We do not show our foot soles when we sit discussing with an Omani. We do not cross our legs. Our hands rest quietly in our lap. The men wear long trousers and a shirt with long sleeves. A jacket is not obligatory, but we often use a tie because we must when on hospital grounds. Our women are properly covered but do not cover their hair.

"When in Rome, do as the Romans do."

Chapter 8

In which one talks about expatriates, a well-educated Arab woman, the ocean, and the forthcoming summer

Indians and other Expatriates

"I have nothing against Indians; I think everybody should have one," one of my English friends said. He has two of them, one for the house and one for the garden. Some have three, the last one for ironing. It is important to have clean, ironed shirts in this heat. You often have to change clothes three times a day.

This country could not function without Indians. There are six hundred thousand Indians here. On top of this, Pakistanis and Filipinos are in significant numbers, as well as a few from Europe and the Americas. We are all expatriates. The Indians have all sorts of jobs. Some are badly paid, but happy. They are happy because they make more money here than at home in India, and because they have work. In the oil drilling camps they live in a fenced area, which they do not leave in two years, it is said. That is usually the period of their contract. They normally do not have their own room. It is not called slavery, but they live under slave-like conditions.

One could say slavery is not a thing of the past. When our dean of the College of Medicine came to this country some ten years ago, there were still slaves in the Dhofar region. They were allowed to drive motorcars and were often well treated, but they could be bought and sold. Rumours say the slave trade is still found at a few places on the Arab peninsula.

My Indian mechanic has three children, a wife, and a sister back in India. He sends a great deal of the money he earns here in Oman back to India to keep them alive and to keep the children in school. Education is so important. He has not seen his family for two years, but hopes that his savings will allow him to go back to India soon for vacation. He has the right to have some weeks' vacation per year. He makes seventy-five rials a months. One tenth of that is for food. His company pays for clothing and transport but not lodging. I make more than two thousand rials per month, so equal opportunities are far away.

Our Indian cleaner, Radu, is happy. His little brother is coming soon. Then there will be two to make money for the family. Lately he got permission to go about the streets in the evening until late. That gives him an opportunity to make a little extra by washing up after parties. He works hard. Many like him have extra jobs, even though they have not got permission from their sponsor.

You have to have a sponsor. Without a sponsor you cannot enter the country. When your sponsor does not need you anymore, you have to leave the country. Women are sent home if they get pregnant before their first two years have elapsed. Many have a husband at home in India. Getting pregnant without a husband? Inconceivable.

The Indian bus driver of our daughter's school bus had several jobs, we were told. One morning he fell asleep behind the wheel while waiting at a red light. The children had to wake him up. Since he was always very tired and his driving was not safe, we complained, knowing he might be returned to India. The next day he was replaced by another Indian, who did not fall asleep.

Life is not always funny, especially if you are a poor expatriate worker without insurance. A worker from Bangladesh was admitted to a local hospital. He had severe bacterial meningitis. Intensive antibiotic treatment resulted in some improvement, and his physicians started to believe he might survive. Then his sponsor arrived. He would not pay for more treatment. The poor man could not pay himself. All treatment was then stopped. The patient was asked to go home to Bangladesh. He could hardly get out of bed. He must have died immediately after.

A British friend has a very bright Indian houseboy. He speaks four languages fluently, including Arabic. He had learned it by listening. At home in India he is rather wealthy, owing some houses and businesses. He has six or seven jobs here in Oman and sends most of his money home to India. He can manage everything, including making a good gin and tonic. He smiles and enjoys life. Recently he had to go to the Indian embassy for business. He talked to the Indian ambassador himself, who treated his application very suspiciously.

"You are only a houseboy," he said with contempt.

Then the "houseboy" became furious. "Sir, I make four hundred rials per months, and that is probably more than you do."

Then His Excellency became silent, because that was true. If the young man had been born into another family in another country he might have become a great man.

Our friend also has a gardener. He takes care of several gardens on campus and is wealthier than most of the Indians here. He owns a rather big farm in Kerela, India, a fertile but poor Indian province. When the mangoes are going to be harvested, this gardener has to employ twenty-five helpers back in India, while he stays here. It is not easy for him. "They ask too much," he said. He earns one rial per hour, and I wonder what he pays his men in India.

An Indian visiting professor told me that his monthly salary was thirty-five times his salary in India. He could also send money back to India.

The banks here are run by Indians. My bank is no exception. The number two in my bank is Mr Anthony. He has a sense of humour and often laughs. But he is worried about the omanisation. The Omanis make too many mistakes, he tells me. That can be serious for the customers, but we all know "The Sultan is right." Omanis must take over jobs in Oman which are presently run by expatriates. When omanisation is complete, in India there will not be nine hundred million Indians but nine million plus the six hundred thousand Indians who are now here.

It seems that after five p.m. they are all assembled on Ruwi High Street, where you can buy everything. My female family members were a bit scared when they saw all those Indians who looked at them hungrily, but any incipient fear disappeared when they realized they could buy Thai silk clothes at one-tenth the price at home.

The business quarters are dominated by Indians. They are not only costumers, they are behind the desks, as grocers, jewellers, tailors, etc. My tailor is also an Indian. He walks softly in his stocking feet. He measures, takes orders. He is in charge of the costumers. His assistant tailors cut and sew. Silence. Like all the Indians I know he is hard working. I want shirts and trousers. "With pleasure," says the kind gentleman. Everything is ready after two days, fitting perfectly. A shirt of the finest material costs one-tenth the price at home. You can also have garments copied. "Same, same." Cheap, cheap. From now on I shall have all my clothes made here. I shall avoid buying any in Europe.

One of my colleagues, a specialist in medical gastroenterology quoted what they say in Savile Row, London, where the expensive tailors live. "A good tailor and good manners are more important than a good education." I am not sure that I agree, but the man who said it is himself well-dressed, and not from Cambridge or Oxford.

The dressmakers are usually Filipinos. Females, of course. Men do not manufacture or sell dresses for women. Oh no, that would be immoral. European ladies come often and in large numbers to the Filipino dressmakers.

The Indians and other Asian expatriates would like their families to join them. But that is impossible. They cannot get a visa. Here the expatriate spouses cannot easily live together, although short visits are permitted, but all low-income expatriates who would like their spouse to come for a short visit must deposit a sum equivalent to the price of a ticket to their home country. Social security is nonexistent, and for foreigners? No, no. I am often asked why refugees from Iraq and Iran do not flee to one of the tolerant Arabic countries rather than to Europe where people do not speak their language. The answer is simple. They will not be let in, unless the refugee has a sponsor who guarantees that the government of Oman will not have to pay in case of disease, and who can guarantee that the refugee has work and can support himself?

The other day I was invited out for dinner. Present was a dark-skinned man named George. This gentleman was chief technologist at one of the laboratories of the university. People often take him for Indian, which he dislikes. He is African. Everybody should be able to see that from his hair, he thinks. He was a refugee from Uganda who somehow ended up in Oman. How, I do not know. His story is this. One day there was an outdoor meeting in Kampala. The president, Idi Amin, was about to speak. He began. The atmosphere was hysteric, as when Adolph Hitler spoke to the Germans before the war. "We want to get rid of the Indians even if Uganda will have to burst into flames," the madman shouted. Everybody was yelling and screaming. Except George. He thought the man was an idiot. Idi Amin spotted him, the only person who remained silent. He pointed at him and asked him to come forward. George disappeared silently in the crowd. The next day he was in Kenya. Idi Amin was known to be able to kill by a well-directed kick. Today one can meet him in the supermarkets in Jedda, Saudi Arabia. He had convinced the Saudi king he was a Muslim, although nobody had noticed that so far. "He has walked about unkilled for a long time," as they said in Iceland a thousand years ago.

George is a happy man. He got his wife and two children out of the country. Now they have ten (they are Catholics). The boys are circumcised; their father did that himself. Nobody died. We have here in Oman every year cases of boys dying from blood loss after circumcision.

It is not difficult to recognize us, the expatriates. None of us will ever be taken for an Omani. Why? Because the Sultan has decided that only Omanis may wear Omani dress. A Sikh wears a special turban, a Pakistani a special cap, a Sudanese something looking like a napkin, and a European or an American wears normal European clothing, sometimes with a straw hat. That is how it is.

The daily life of this country is influenced by the British and the English language. It is well known that His Majesty is an anglophile. British military helped him to suppress a rebellion in the not-too-distant past. The British have trained the Omani army, navy, air force, and police. This country still has warm relations with Great Britain. The British ambassador is a nice man and a very important person here. I have met and talked to him (we have common British friends). There are a few thousand British residents here. Quite a number of those are employed by the university and the major hospitals. As in the United Kingdom, the titles are military. For example, a head nurse is called senior nursing officer. There are always two swing doors, one for incoming traffic and one for outgoing. It is important to choose the left one, as in England, to avoid a traffic jam. However, the Sultan a long time ago decided that in Oman, one drives on the right side of the road. The roads and motorways are built by the Germans, but all road signs are in English and Arabic. All official letters are bilingual, but recently they began to write telephone bills in Arabic only. Luckily I can read Arabic numbers.

Most of the postgraduate education for Omanis takes place in England and Canada, not in the United States, which has less influence here than the British, except for the military. There are quite a few Dutch people here because of the oil and gas, which is exploited by the Dutch-dominated Shell. Most flights to Oman are performed by British Airways and KLM.

There a few Scandinavians working here: very few Norwegians, around seventy-five Swedes, and around seventy-five Danes. Most of the Swedes are employed by the university. Our Swedish is improving. It is a beautiful language, also for singing. Denmark has a vice consul, a man younger than my youngest son. His job might not be easy. His resources are few.

Why do people from Europe come to Oman in order to work? There are three main reasons: divorce, taxes, and unemployment. Those are perhaps not ideal causes, but the European expatriates working here are mostly well qualified and perform well. There are people working here who have come for special reasons, such as love of adventure. I know one, a male American technologist who works one year in every country which wants him on his way around the globe. He recommends Samoa, if you can stand humid, warm temperatures and ants eating your wooden house in a week. Another one, an English professor of paediatrics, left his country because he was tired of writing applications to private foundations in order to raise money to run his department. He thought correctly that his hospital should pay whatever necessary to run his department. They do here.

Many of the expatriates I have met here are tired of the over-administered Europe and the foreign immigrants who cannot support themselves. Here in Oman we also have immigrants and expatriates, but they (we) work. Oman is popular among people who know the Middle East. Although the wages are not as impressive as in Saudi Arabia, living is inexpensive, we do not pay tax, the Omanis are tolerant and friendly, and we feel safe here. Some come to Oman from other Arab countries due to fundamentalism, which is an increasing problem in the Arab world.

Here is a true story from an Arab country with a fundamentalist Muslim opposition: A high-ranking police officer had received several anonymous threats. The last one informed him that he would die the first coming Wednesday. He stayed home that day. He arranged for police protection. His colleagues surrounded the house. Lunch was served by his wife. The grown-up son living with his parents joined them as usual for lunch. Exactly at noon he stands op, draws a pistol, and says to his father, "Your time has come," and kills him with one shot in his head. Then he leaves the house in order to tell his superior in his fundamentalist movement that he obeyed orders. His superior asked whether anybody saw him. "Nobody except my mother, and she will say nothing," he replied. Then he was ordered to go back and shoot his mother, which he did.

We have had some university teachers and physicians from Kuwait. Two colleagues were in Europe on vacation when Saddam Hussein invaded Kuwait. They lost all their possessions. They had to start from scratch, middle aged as they were, not far from retirement. One of them went back to Kuwait after the war. His possessions were gone; he found nothing, not even a teaspoon. The Emir of Kuwait, having come back after others had saved his country, decided to compensate Westerners, if they had had money in the bank. Our colleague came back to Oman empty handed, apart from some money.

The Gulf War was tough. The Saudis are consequent people. When they noticed that Yemen supported Saddam Hussein, after the Gulf War they expelled all Yeminis working in Saudi Arabia, around half a million people, who now became unemployed. Their jobs were taken over by Indians. The Saudis themselves do not like manual work. This exodus contributed to the augmentation of poverty in Yemen, which was already one of the poorest countries in the world. However, recently oil companies have found rather big quantities of oil in Yemen. Maybe Yemen is facing a Renaissance, like Oman did twenty-five years ago. The tribal wars may then stop, like they did in Oman. For the time being travelling to Yemen seems dangerous. There are highwaymen who steal lorries and rob people, taking everything except their pants. An America doctor who is helping American citizens in Sana'a, the capital of Yemen, told us of the incredibly low status of medical services in Yemen. After the Gulf War they do not even have a hospital there. The hospitals they once had were financed by Saudi Arabia and Kuwait. After the Gulf War, the stream of money suddenly stopped.

For the time being, many Westerners stop working in Saudi Arabia and go home. The Saudis are short on cash. The oil prices are falling. We hear of people who have not been paid for three months. They leave without the cash they should have had and without their bonus, the bonus being cancelled when you leave before the scheduled expiry date in your contract.

It is also becoming more dangerous for Westerners in Saudi Arabia. The nurse who arrived in Oman at the same time as we did relaxed. She did not have to be afraid anymore. Oman is a free country. No Mutawas. In Saudi Arabia they interfere with the daily life of Westerners. The nurse said there was a party in an embassy of a Western non-Muslim country. This party took place on a piece of land which was not Saudi Arabia. However, a bunch of Mutawas broke in, beating up the guests, believing they drank alcohol, which they did not. All the guests ran to their cars trying to escape. A wife of a diplomat was severely beaten up and lost an eye. The Mutawas walked away.

It became worse after the Gulf War. One must say the Americans are not always smart. They came to Saudi Arabia with female soldiers in shorts and shirts with short sleeves, showing a lot of bare skin, in Saudi Arabia, the most orthodox Muslim country in the world. Not good. One day it was too much for the Mutawas. They approached a hut housing the female warriors. They and their sticks were ready for beating up the American women, presumptuous womenfolk. In the doorway a female officer appeared in shorts and short sleeves, hands on her tempting hips, pistol in her belt. She shouted, "If you come closer, I shoot." They did come closer, and she did shoot, killing one of the Mutawas. The next day she was in Germany.

I am glad I am not in Saudi Arabia these days but that I was there in more peaceful times.

An Unusual Woman

There are many interesting people on campus. Haddia is one of them, a lady who is difficult to forget. She is a divorcee with three grown-up children, two sons and a daughter. Haddia is a daughter of an imam in Algiers, a learned man of integrity and tolerance. He had only one wife, and they had a number of children who were all successful in life. They now help each other when it is needed. Haddia has two university degrees, one in physics and one in medicine. She works in four departments: the department of medical physics, the department of nuclear medicine, the department of medicine, and the department of physiology and clinical physiology. In all departments she does research.

Recently she was promoted to consultant. This was an opportunity to have a little party. Haddia did the cooking, sixteen courses. She started in the morning by shopping and worked the whole day in the kitchen. The children were servants.

She ought to be senior consultant by now. But she is a woman, and she is a divorcee. Haddia speaks, reads, and writes Arabic, French, and English fluently. She does it fast; often the languages are mixed so that she in one sentence uses words from all three. This is very charming. Haddia works at her departments ten hours per day and then after supper another couple of hours while the kids do the washing up and their homework. Never a dull moment. Sometimes in the morning there is time for a little swim, and perhaps a little jogging late in the evening. She is very fast on a PC. Sometimes she makes mistakes and she exclaims, "Merde." The patients love her. She is producing lots of data. She knows mathematics and physics, two disciplines which are extremely important in medical research.

The other day I said to her after she had been completing our last article from two to seven a.m.: "Haddia, you are rather ambitious, I think," to which she replied, "No, my main concern is the future of my children."

That is probably true. For many years she has spent two-thirds of her salary on the children's education. The British-American Academy is expensive. "Money is no problem," she says. "You can live on very little if you know where to shop."

Contrary to the Westerners, the family does not spend money on alcoholic beverages, but she has nothing against serving "un champagne Algerien," meaning soda water mixed with apple juice.

Haddia has two sons, sixteen and eighteen years old, and a daughter of twenty years. The elder son is described elsewhere in this book. He is the one with the best A-levels in the history of Oman. When he was a little boy, his head looked rather big. The local paediatrician suggested an operation to find out if there was too much water inside (hydrocephalus). "We have to open it up to see what is wrong," he said. This was before the time of CT scans.

The mother knew what was wrong. What was wrong was that the paediatrician did not know what he was talking about. Haddia left with her son and did not return to the incompetent colleague. The mother could see the boy was unusually intelligent. One day, shortly after he had learned to walk, his sister was stuck behind the sofa and could not get out. The little boy threw one cushion after the other behind the sofa so that his sister could climb out. You do not reason like that if you have hydrocephalus.

When the boy was three his mother needed somebody to look after him, since the maid had stopped, and Haddia had to go to work. She asked her daughter's teacher if her three-year-old could sit in the classroom for a couple of weeks until a new maid was found. That was all right. He sat there for some weeks listening to the big children reading and writing Arabic. They were given homework. The boy was tired when he was picked up in the afternoon. He fell asleep after dinner. In the morning he got out of bed one hour before the others. Then he sat on his knees in a chair doing his homework. After a couple of weeks practice, he could read the newspaper.

Soon he will leave his family to go to America where he will begin his career as a student at the renowned MIT (Massachusetts Institute of Technology), being the first student ever from Oman to have gained access to this famous institution. The mother travels with him to make sure he starts well. She is relaxed, although there are strong anti-Arabic sentiments in the United States. Did the boy get his visa or not? In the Arab world, a lot can be done when you have *wasda,* meaning "influence" (he has an uncle who is a diplomat). The daughter is studying in Paris, and the younger brother is still at the British-American Academy in Muscat, like my daughter.

The children always helped their mother at home. Sometimes they earned a little money by working in a library. They gave their mother that money. They kept nothing for themselves. At the dinner table scientific subjects are discussed. The family does not possess a TV. That would be a waste of time. But they have computers and printers. I praised her children and told her how impressed I was by her as a mother and physician. She replied in

English with her characteristic French accent, "Everything went well with the help of God, Alhamdulillah" (Allah be praised).

The Ocean

Oman is by the Indian Ocean. Our fishery biologists tell us that nowhere on this globe is the fauna so rich as here. After having snorkelled or dived a couple of times, I believe it. Since there are so many fishes there are also many sea birds. And whales are abundant, many different kinds of whales. They are difficult to distinguish because we often see them at a distance from a boat. Once a whale was twenty meters from our boat. Whether they are dangerous when they come closer we don't know.

The water is never too cold. In February it is usually around twenty-five degrees Celsius, ideal for swimming. The underwater world is extremely beautiful. Colourful fishes and corals. Often one can encounter corals one meter under the surface in otherwise deep waters, but we don't stand on them, because that could ruin their growth which is very slow. Among the fishes are sharks, big ones and small ones. The big ones look dangerous, but there are no reports from these waters that humans have been attacked by sharks, but we know people who had been frightened by a big shark when swimming, thereafter hurrying back to their boat. One of our female friends tried that. She almost walked on the water to get back to the boat quickly. One colleague photographed a ten-meter shark with yellow eyes. It did not attack. There are fishes enough for the sharks, so they do not have to eat humans.

We also have stingrays. They can be a couple of meters in size. One of my colleagues thought he was standing on sand. Suddenly he was lifted up. It was an enormous stingray. They have their name, because on the middle of the upside part of the tail they have a poisonous hook which they use to defend themselves when attacked. A Danish eye doctor is fascinated by stingrays. He tells us that when meeting a stingray underwater, we should grasp the end of its tail, and the stingray will take us on to an interesting underwater tour. Our daughter was stung by one when she was sitting on her knees in shallow water. She was taken to the emergency department of the hospital, had pain, and there was a wound. Her blood pressure was low. The Filipino nurses would give her morphine which would have lowered her blood pressure further. I prevented that and she recovered in a few hours.

The sea snakes are more dangerous. We have seen them a couple of times on the surface of deep water, but they can also be seen in shallow water. One bite and you are dead in a few seconds. Luckily for us they cannot open their mouths wide, but they can bite the skin between your fingers. Then there are poisonous sea urchins, moray eels, and life-threatening, stinging jellyfish, but apart from those creatures, swimming here is wonderful, and we do it often.

The turtles are interesting. The adults are big. They can reach an age of three hundred years. They lay their eggs on the beach at night, if they are not disturbed by tourists.

Hunting underwater is not permitted. Some people have a certificate allowing them to do SCUBA diving, but even they are not allowed to kill by spear or catch the big lobsters that taste good. Tuna is caught by hook, a wonderful sport, which was popular among rich Danes when I was a kid. Now the mackerel has disappeared from Danish waters, and therefore the tuna. But in Oman they are abundant, and they are inexpensive to buy.

The nets create problems for the boats, but we take care. The whales do not like them and some have lost their lives because of the nets. Now there is a voluntary whale-rescue group who turn out when a whale is stuck. They have saved many whales.

The diving Westerners have been learning to dive at the Diving Centre. If they get decompression sickness they can be treated. It is now possible to treat this condition with hyperbaric oxygen, even in this country.

The fishermen have begun to make big money. Giant freezers are being installed. Lorries for transport of cooled fish are now in operation. Some drive to the interior, so that the villagers there can get fresh fish, while others drive to neighbouring countries such as Saudi Arabia. Some are transported by air to Europe. We buy fish at the fish market in Seeb, a fishing village not far from the university, often directly from the boats when they get ashore. We prefer tuna and kingfish. A nice, middle-sized tuna can be purchased at a price of one rial. When we do that, we have food for a week. We can also buy squid and octopus and giant prawns, but then we have to go to the fish market in Muttrah, a fantastic place with a variety of fish on display, fish that we do not know. Sole, which is so delicious and expensive in Europe, is very cheap here, where for some odd reason it is not popular. We have not tasted all fifty species for sale, but one thing is clear: Oman is a place where you can eat good fish.

When you walk on the beach here you can walk for hours without seeing a human being. But you will see a multitude of mussels, big and small ones, colourful or white, unusual shapes. The physician Doctor Don Bosch has written a beautifully illustrated book on the mussels of Oman titled "Seashells of Oman". He had the Sultan and members of the Royal Family as his patients. He is very popular in this country, living after his retirement in the villa which was given to him by the Sultan. Naturally it is on the beach, beautifully situated. What can one learn from this story? Grateful patients exist.

Sailing and boating are popular sports among Westerners. It is not always without risk to move around on the Omani waters. Two young Europeans had problems with their engine far from the coast. The engine stopped, and would not start again. They came ashore after days and found themselves on a beach in Iran. After having been arrested, accused of espionage, they spent some time in an Iranian prison, an experience they said was very unpleasant. We are glad our friend Nick has two engines. We have witnessed one of them stopped near the Demanyat Islands. I once asked him whether he was afraid of ending up in Iran. He is not. Although he has no compass, he knows his way back: when the sun hits his right lower leg on the way home at two p.m. he knows he is on the right track. Luckily the sun shines almost every day. I am only nervous when it is hazy.

If we against expectations should end up in Iran, we have the advantage that Nicks speaks Farsi.

Summer

Summer has arrived. It is not nice. I no longer open the window when shaving in the morning. The cold tap water is now so hot that it is it is no longer possible to take a cold shower. It has also become difficult to be a housewife. You have to use the cold water from the fridge when rinsing salad. The tap water destroys the salad. The cicadas sing so loudly they deafen you.

Many colleagues have temporarily returned to Europe or Canada or wherever they used to live, because it is cooler there. I cannot walk the five hundred meters to the hospital but have to take the car. The outdoor temperature has not yet reached fifty degrees Celsius. At midday it is only forty-five degrees. Officially the temperature never goes above fifty because work stops all over the Sultanate if the temperature in the shade exceeds fifty. That is the law. It was, however, fifty-five degrees Celsius (this is one hundred thirty degrees Fahrenheit) when we arrived here, but everybody worked. Our daughter is loaded with water when she goes to the school bus in the morning. The children don't leave the classrooms during the daytime.

Our friend Nick and his wife had also decided to go to Europe. I took them to the airport. Nick was in high spirits. He almost always is. His wife said, "Nick is inappropriately happy. He has every reason to be unhappy: He is overweight, drinks too much, and has a neurotic wife." He has now come back to Oman after his holiday and is still happy and content. Perhaps it has something to do with the fact that he has never paid tax. He does not know how.

The other day, when we were in Salalah, there was a power outage on campus for twelve hours. An Indian worker had hit an electric cable while digging with his excavator. He is said to have been killed instantly but was immediately replaced. What concerned the people living on campus was the fact that everything in their fridge and deep freeze was destroyed. Worse was there were no ice cubes for the drinks before dinner. The air conditioning stopped. Children and adults could not sleep. Many left campus if they knew people outside who could produce ice cubes for their drinks.

Sleeping is difficult without air conditioning. People here do not know the trick from Malaysia. Sleep under wet sheets wrung out in chilled water.

One day we did not take the midday sun seriously, although Kipling had taught us to do so. My daughter and I drove in our car to the supermarket ten kilometres away. Suddenly the engine stopped. There was an unpleasant smell, like a dead rat. We had forgotten water and hats but started to walk to the supermarket, although we soon realized we should have stayed in the shade. A number of cars with Arab drivers passed by. When we were on the brink of fainting, an old car with a British driver stopped. This driver could see we had problems with the merciless glare of the sun at its in zenith. We could not see our own shadow.

That day taught us to bring water and cover our heads, even when on a short trip.

Most birds have migrated to cooler areas. Those left behind do not sing anymore. Now the oleanders in the wadis do not blossom. Plants and trees are now resting, waiting for cooler times. It is too hot. However, there are exceptions, such as the flame trees which now blossom with orange-red flowers. They are extremely beautiful. I saw a big one which had cracked due to the weight of its flowers.

The Omanis do not sweat to the extent we do. Recently I sat in the canteen watching a young Omani woman. She was extremely beautiful, and looked as if the high temperature did not bother her. David, our superintendent, noticed the direction of my eyes, and said, "Don't do that, Pors. You might have your reproductive tackle chopped off.". David has a rich vocabulary. He could paint with his English words. I followed his advice and looked at an elderly woman instead. My reproductive tackle is intact.

Those of the colleagues who stayed here and did not go to Europe or Canada drove to the Hajar mountains on weekends. The temperatures there even in midsummer can be almost agreeable. One weekend we had planned to go to the Jabel Shams, the highest mountain in the country. It was cancelled due to other arrangements. The others went off and to their surprise had lots of rain. One car had to wait for five hours to pass a wadi with streaming water. We have tried that too.

Instead I went to paint at a place near Al Khod, where I had painted before. Now I wanted to paint the same motif again. The light is always different, and as the famous French painters Claude Monet and Edgar Degas had noticed, sometimes the paintings become better if the motif is painted more than once. I had to stop after a couple of hours due to the heat. I must say that I prefer painting to camping. It is relaxing to paint. Although I do not suffer from stress, which incidentally is not a disease, but a symptom, I understand what Winston Churchill said shortly before his death, "If it weren't for painting I couldn't bear the strain of things." During the war though, it went quite well without painting.

He only painted one picture during the war. That was in Marrakech, where he sat in his hotel high up painting the Atlas Mountains, which can be seen from there with their snow-covered peaks. I have been there recently. The scenery is beautiful. The paralyzed American President Franklin D. Roosevelt was carried to the top of the building to meet the painting British prime minister. Churchill later gave him the picture, which is now in the White House ("Churchill and Roosevelt met in Marrakech 1944 after the British-American invasion in North-West Africa").

The landscapes here in Oman are so beautiful that they should attract painters from all over the world. The interest in going out to paint is increasing in Oman, also among young Omanis. Art exhibitions are arranged, and people come. The mountains are beautiful in the morning light, but they are also strikingly beautiful in the late-afternoon light. However, I find it too difficult to paint when the light changes too swiftly. I know very well that Claude Monet often had six canvasses in a row, so that he could catch the changing light, but I have not yet come that far.

Today is the thirty-first of May, and tomorrow the Scandinavian summer begins. Here it is New Year's day, the first day in the new Arab year, the first Muharram 1416 AH. It came one day sooner than expected. The Moon Sighting Committee must have been meeting again. It was said on TV and radio that the new moon had been sighted. That settled the matter. How lucky there were no clouds. The teachers had to phone the parents of the schoolchildren to tell them the boys and girls should not come to school tomorrow because New Year had arrived.

Another couple of weeks have elapsed. In a few days the school will close for the summer. Our daughter received a prize as the pupil who had made the most pronounced progress during the school year. She has occasional problems with her Danish. She did not believe me when I said: "It is called *kompliceret*, not *complicated*."

The temperature reached forty-nine degrees yesterday when I met one of my British colleagues on campus. He said, "I don't think we shall have snow today." The British can always talk about the weather. He was right. We did not have snow. It is now impossible to go barefoot on the terrace. That would give you second-degree burns.

It is time for summer holiday in Denmark

Chapter 9

In which one looks at the past and future and visits Jabal Shams to avoid the heat, after which one says good-bye.

The Past

It was green and cool in Denmark. Occasional rain. Wonderful. After a short summer vacation, I am back in Muscat. Here on the Batinah Coast it is, however, unbearably hot and humid, more humid than earlier, because now it is monsoon season in the south. In India they wait for the monsoon. People there die in their hundreds every day from heat stroke. It is like that every year. A policeman in New Delhi complained that he had to spend one-third of his salary on water and juices in order to be able to direct the traffic.

Today is 23 July 1995. It is an important day, being the twenty-fifth anniversary of the Sultan's ascension to the throne. We wonder if we shall have one month extra salary. That was given to everybody at the twentieth anniversary, but it is said that this time the government has to cut down on expenses.

Allah's birthday present to His Majesty was an unexpectedly long-lasting rain over northern Oman. Now everybody could see that His Majesty is something special. What had happened, and that is unusual, was that the monsoon had moved further north than usual, apparently due to a cyclone far away.

As expected, today's newspapers concentrate on the anniversary. They all had a special anniversary supplement, dealing exclusively with the outstanding qualities of His Majesty. The supplements were tributes to the great leader of the country, paid by advertisements of the main businesses of Oman. Every newspaper had a whole-page advertisement from the Finance Minister. He and his family own one of the most successful business empires in the country. The different firms owned by the great man and his brothers were lined up. The Finance Minister might have been chosen for the job because he is a shrewd businessman. Every time I go shopping in my supermarket, I think of the Finance Minister while contributing to the growth of his personal fortune. If this regime one day will be finished, it might be because of the private businesses of the ministers. It must be difficult to dissociate private and governmental interests.

The newspapers are full of Oman in the old days and now, about the Renaissance twenty-five years ago, and the progress of the last twenty-five years.

Last year, 1994, was appointed to the year of preservation of the cultural inheritance of Oman. People abroad should not believe Oman is devoid of a cultural past. That is not the case. Some years ago I said to a well-known professor in London that I was fascinated by Arab culture. He looked at me, and betraying his ignorance, said, "You mean lack of culture?" No, I did not. When people in Europe believed the world ended in the countries around the Mediterranean and that the earth was flat like a pancake, for which reason one should be careful not to approach its edge, Omani sailors sailed in their dhows to China, India, and what is now Indonesia, directed by nautical instruments invented and constructed by themselves. They lived in busy cities and had a highly developed culture, spreading along the coasts of Persia, the Gulf, and East Africa. This vast empire without an emperor was only destroyed when the Portuguese managed to sail south of Africa, whereby the trade in and around Oman was reduced.

Many of the Omani mosques are very old, but there are few traces of the early Islamic period. However, it is known how Oman became an Islamic country. The region of present day Oman was the first one to convert to

Islam. It happened without the use of the sword, which was unusual. The Prophet later said, "Blessed be Ghubaira [the old name for Oman, still used in Zanzibar], for they believed in me without having seen me."

The Prophet Mohammed, Allah's messenger, who lived in what is now Saudi Arabia, had sent almost identical letters to the heads of state of the surrounding countries, the East Roman emperor in Constantinople included.

Here is his letter to Oman:

"In God's name, he the most merciful, from Mohammed, God's messenger to Jaifar and Abd, sons of al-Julanda [they governed in common]. Peace be upon those who adhere to the true faith. Be greeted. I encourage you to convert to Islam. Embrace Islam, and you shall be redeemed because I am God's messenger for all mankind. I have come to warn all living. Suffering shall be the fate of the infidels. If you embrace Islam, everything will be good. If not, your kingdom shall disappear, and my horses will trample you to death, and my faith shall triumph."

Oman converted. The branch of Islam prevailing here is Ibadism, a very old orthodox kind of Islam. Moderation and tolerance have always been its hallmark, although this country has had its fanatical periods. However, according to my historical sources, one can say Oman has been dominated by Puritanism without fanaticism. That can be seen in the mosques, old ones and new. They are plain, not decorated, unlike in other parts of the Arab world.

There are Shiites and Sunnis in the coastal areas, and the country is not free of religious tensions, but clever men say it is worse in some other countries not far away. According to handed-down reports, St. Thomas brought Christianity to Oman. Before Islam there were, for six hundred years in Oman, many Christians, bishops included. There were also rather many Jews, and until a few years ago there was a Jewish community in Sohar. Islam was tolerant at the beginning, treated Jews and Christians well, like in Spain. When the Portuguese came five hundred years ago, they did not treat the Muslims that well.

When Jesus lived, at the time when the Roman Empire dominated all the countries of the Mediterranean, there was also a buzz of activity in Persia and Oman. The city of Sohar is situated at the sea in the northern part of the country, not far from the Straits of Hormuz. Then it was four times larger than today. Some years ago a giant gold treasure was found there, including a jarful of Roman gold coins with the portrait of the Roman Emperor Tiberius. He governed from 14 to 35 AD. Does that mean there was trade between Oman and Rome? Most likely. How else would the Romans get frankincense? It is possible Roman coins were a sort of international currency, like US dollars today.

The Omanis later showed they appreciate money. During the last two hundred years, Omanis have used the Maria Theresa thaler (MTT), an Austrian silver coin from the eighteenth century. The British government decided to produce some of those coins for Oman. They sent the money by ship to Oman during the Second World War. Unfortunately, the ship was sunk by a German submarine. The other day I went to the fishing village Seeb to buy fish for the coming days. It was Thursday, and on Thursdays there is a market there. Outside the local soukh sat three sheiks from the Interior. They looked worthy with their kunjars, sitting on an Omani rug. In front of them were stacked a column of Maria Theresa thalers. They have not accepted the Sultan's paper money. The men were remnants of olden times, dealing in rifles, mainly old Winchesters with silver plates, as they had done for many years.

Oman's history goes further back than to the time of Jesus two thousand years ago, although written sources before Jesus are scarce. However, pre-Islamic scriptures can be seen in Samhuram near Salalah in the Dhofar region. They are very old. To me the letters look like the Nordic runic letters. It appears that when they were written, people worshipped the moon god Sin of ancient Mesopotamia.

Excavations have recently resulted in the finding of hundreds of arrowheads, spearheads, and jewellery from 3000 BC. Last year, near Ras Al Hamra they found the remnants of a six thousand- year-old city.

The most sensational find in later years has been the discovery of the ancient city of Umar in the Dhofar region. This city is described in the Holy Koran as the city with many columns, the likes of which is not found in the whole world. It was discovered by a person looking at some satellite photos. He saw some regular structures and straight lines irradiating from there. Archaeologists had been searching for it over the years. It was known to have been the centre of the frankincense trade for centuries. Suddenly it was there with roads, pieces of columns, walls, foundations, etc. Some of the stones examined were seven thousand years old. Those of our colleagues who have been there say that there is not much to see, but we see less than the archaeologists. Their excavations are going on.

The Future

His Majesty made some speeches on the occasion of the twenty-fifth anniversary. The subjects varied, but there was invariably something about the future. The poor man must everyday think of the possibility that the future of his country might not include him. He might be assassinated. Arab leaders are often killed. One of the topics of his speeches was the Majlis Ash'shura, which is going to increase its influence in the future. He made it possible for women to be elected. There are already a number of female members of this consultative board. You cannot see a bit of hair in their face in front of their scarf.

The Sultan said, concerning the permission for women to become members of this consultative assembly, "This step is a correction of a misunderstanding, which has led to the belief that women are inferior to men. This is not the case. The country needs all hands for its development and stability." A courageous statement.

His Majesty made a clever decision when he did not nationalize the oil industry in spite of advice from many clever men. They did in Iran, and that was not a success. They perhaps are going to change that decision, but one never knows with Persians. For Oman, the decision not to nationalize the oil industry meant heaps of foreign capital. Hopefully all shall go well. It did not for the Shah of Persia.

Oman might have a substantiated hope that the country will succeed, even when oil will be depleted thirty years from now. Firstly, His Majesty has made it possible for the people of Oman to be educated. That has been widely neglected in some other Arab countries. Secondly, one has not focused only on oil. There are in this country minerals such as copper, chromium, gold, silver, etc. And there is coal, something India is interested in buying for the old coal-burning locomotives, relics from the time of British India. Also, fishes can be pleased that the Sultan is so wise. He has decided the sea shall not be emptied of fish in the near future.

On the other hand, whether it shall all go well for Oman when the oil and gas revenues are declining, the population is increasing, and there will still be oil and gas in the Emirates and Saudi Arabia, is difficult to know. One of our colleagues, who has been in the Middle East for many years, said rather cynically, "Loyalty in the Middle East is something that can be bought and sold." If the price is better in neighbouring countries, problems of social unrest here are likely to come. The truth is it became easier to unite the country when oil was being produced in big quantities.

At the university, we often discuss the growth of the population. At the moment (1995), a doubling of the population in fifteen years is foreseen. Changes are rapid here and in the other Arab countries. Overpopulation is not a matter of the future. It is already here. We in the West should not sell our medical expertise the way we do. For the time being, we are highly responsible for the population explosion here. We make sure infant mortality decreases, and we cure diseases which used to be lethal. What we should say to governments wanting our assistance is, "You can have our help, but you must take all of it, birth control included." Without birth control, everything goes wrong: there will be wars, diseases, and ethnic cleansing, like in Rwanda and Burundi, where the main problem was that the population was too big to be supported, too big relative to the cultivated area.

It may be that our planet will begin to defend itself against the human race, which is destroying it. Perhaps AIDS or some other virus solves the overpopulation problem. A colleague returning from some months in Africa tells about villages totally annihilated by the AIDS crisis. We have faced the consequences of infectious diseases before. During the Middle Ages, the plague halved the populations in some European countries. Now about half the soldiers in Zimbabwe have AIDS. In Zaire and Uganda, there are districts where 80 per cent of all pregnant women are HIV-positive.

The Omanis can rejoice. Apart from oil, gas, and minerals, they have areas of fertile farmland, which, however, sometimes is difficult to exploit because of lack of water. In all Arab countries, water shortage is a problem. Some say shortage of water will become a cause of war in the near future. Irrigation is common in Oman. We see many wells, also in the coastal areas. Here there are so many wells that saltwater comes in and destroys the water quality in the wells, and the palms die. This year, large amounts of fossil water has been found to the joy of all Omanis, but that of course is only a temporary pleasure.

However, other means of improving the water situation exist. It is well known that on rare occasions when it rains in the mountains, there is a lot of water coming down. Much water evaporates before it can seep into the ground, and some water is wasted running into the ocean. However, the Water Conservation Ministry has begun to build dams for preservation of the water which otherwise would have ended up in the ocean. More dams could be built. A dam might mean the difference between life and death for a small community. That was seen when many years ago the Marib Dam in Yemen broke down. When that happened, a flourishing culture disappeared, a culture which peaked when the Queen of Sheba was alive and ruling the country.

In the future, desalination will probably be used more extensively, if energy is available. It is here, even when there will be no more oil, because gas is believed to last longer. Recently, more gas has been found. The Japanese helped, and have offered to buy some of the gas in frozen form. The Sultan has plans of a gas tube to India. And then there is solar energy. I have not yet understood why this non-polluting form of energy is not exploited more intensively in this country where there is sun almost every day.

It is nice to be in a place where there is optimism and progress, but one shivers when thinking of the population explosion.

Jabal Shams

The mountains are far away, shades of blue and brown in the morning light. They ask me every morning when I greet them, "Why don't you come visit soon?" I decided to go. I now did what I for a long time had wanted to do. I fled from the heat and went to the northern Al Hajar Mountains.

I departed with Allan, a Brit working as a senior consultant in internal medicine. After us came Joe and his wife in another car, and at last our two Swedish gynaecologists.

After a couple of hours it went steeply upwards. We had with us a detailed British military map, acquired back in England. Apart from that we had a satellite-navigation system (GPS) assisting us in finding our designated goal. This tiny thing developed by the US military can in its civil version take its user to the chosen destination wherever on the Globe within a radius of twenty meters. The coordinates of the goal are entered. The display tells us the distance and gives us the height above sea level. We can also see the calculated time needed to get there. (The military GPS, which is used for cruise missiles and other interesting purposes, has an uncertainty of a couple of centimetres, using more satellites than ours.)

We got exactly where Allan wanted us to go at the calculated time.

The GPS device is useful in the desert and at sea, especially if you have a cell phone or a radio transmitter. You can send your coordinates to the outside world so you can be picked up.

We passed two cities lying in ruins, relics of the recent unrest in the Interior during the reign of the father of the present Sultan. There was a civil war going on. The Sultan could not manage the conservative, very religious inhabitants in the city of Nizwa and its surroundings. This city has for centuries been a centre for orthodox Muslims and residence for the Imam. The Royal Air Force offered its assistance in solving the problem. They told the citizens that two cities were to be bombed the next day, so if they would, please leave the city. The cities were evacuated and thereafter destroyed by bombing, but there were no injuries. Hereafter there were no problems with the people of the area, but there were nests of resistance and a few resistance fighters holding the top of a tall mountain with very steep slopes. We passed that mountain. I would not like to climb its walls. A British elite military group, the special air service (SAS) did something in the middle of the night that was supposed to be impossible, they climbed the mountain. No British soldiers were killed. The leaders of the resistance fighters escaped and now live in Jeddah, Saudi Arabia.

Unfortunately one cannot get to the top of Jabal Al Shams, the tallest mountain of the country, 3009 metres above sea level, situated in the middle of the Jabal Al Akhdar massif. At the peak is a military radar station being able to reveal all of importance on the Arab peninsula. It can observe events on the Russian side of the Black Sea. The British Royal Air Force is said to run it, but officially it is of course Omani military.

Less than Jabal Shams would do. The mountain peaks were all breathtakingly beautiful. It was not easy to drive on the gravel roads of the mountain slopes. They had almost disappeared during the rain of the Ascension Day, that day when Allah had decided to show the world that Sultan Qaboos had his special favour. It had been a blessing rain. And there was enough of it. Now, more than a week after the rain, the wadis were full of clean, streaming water. Trees and bushes blossomed – that is, if they had not died from lack of water before the rain.

We were done in from driving the car on bad roads. At our designated place we were met by a very powerful smell of jasmine coming from trees (*qasam* in Arabic). So far it has no Latin name. I liked the smell.

I placed my camping bed there. It appeared that not only I but also thousands of flies liked the smell. They rested on my skin, making it very difficult to sleep. But I enjoyed the silence and the soft breeze. Next time I shall remind myself that Allah did not make the smell for us but for the continuation of the species.

There were also mosquitoes and midges. My colleagues thought there might be a risk of acquiring malaria here, but that the risk was insignificant.

Not being able to sleep, I watched the stars, which were more beautiful than elsewhere. That I knew from Saudi Arabia. Allan told me of an astronomical computer program, which shared that in the year 2 BC, Jupiter and Venus were superimposed, producing in the Middle East apparently one very big shining star. Everybody must be able to understand that when the male and female planets are superimposed, something special must be going on. This must have been the Star of Bethlehem, meaning Jesus was born two years earlier than we had assumed. Perhaps one should trust astronomers more than verbal traditions. The story of the birth of Jesus was written many years later. He has probably himself not known his birthday. Even now, here in the Middle East, it is common that elderly people do not know when they were born. It is not important. By the way, here in Oman it is common to believe the three wise men from the East described in the Bible came from the Dhofar region of present Oman. After all, they came with gold, frankincense, and myrrh, which are all found in the Dhofar region.

We rose early in the morning because the temperature is agreeable in the morning. To metres from my bare feet was a five-centimetre scorpion doing his last walk before hiding in order to protect himself from the rising sun. I was on my way to the car, where I had placed my shoes to avoid scorpions crawling into them. We learned that in Saudi Arabia. I took a couple of photos before it slipped away into hiding under its stone.

A scorpion feeds on insects. It grabs the prey between its two powerful pincers. Then comes its poisonous tail from above, the sting, and the insect is dead. The scorpion then waits half an hour before it devours it. All this

I know from a colleague who had a scorpion as a pet, a strange hobby. It was called Wilfred until it gave birth to twenty tiny scorpions. From that day it was named Wilfrida.

Adults don't die after having been stung by a scorpion. It hurts, and there is a local reaction, which will wear off. Babies can, however, die from a scorpion sting. Fearing scorpions and snakes, we always wear real shoes when walking here. People who live here don't, they wear sandals and the children go barefoot(!). That we saw later that morning when some children and adults came to sell us homemade rugs. The adults were women and old men. They spin while walking, using wool from their own goats. The rugs smell from goat and are rather coarse.

The women are often alone with the children. Their men travel, take casual jobs, coming home in between, impregnate their women, and depart again. The women are alone most of the time. As a result, they are very independent. They are not veiled and not afraid of talking to us. We are not allowed to take their photo. "*Mafi* pictures," they say ("No pictures").

Without their goats, they could not survive. They grow nothing. I thought of the Bible, of women fetching water from the well. Elsewhere in Jabel Akhdar they grow roses, apricots, plums, apples, and a variety of vegetables.

It is obvious that the men are away, because somebody has to make money when farming is not possible. It was like that on the Danish Island of Læsø in the old days. There the women were very independent. They inherited the farm, married, and the husband had to make his living from sailing far away from home. Some never came back, and others came home after four or five years abroad and found the family had been blessed by two more children. They had a good vicar …

The Jebel people are well trained and slim. They walk a lot. The old men are shepherds and walk all the time. The women too. Two young women came from the village three kilometres away. They were around eighteen years old, exceedingly beautiful, with colourful dresses and classical silver jewellery, wearing laundry on their heads and carrying water jars in their hands. After them came six children. They were all on their way to the spring, which was four hundred meters down in the "Grand Canyon," the big ravine near Jabal Shams, which is even more impressive than the American one. We were having lunch under an old olive tree, the diameter of its trunk being three meters. A stone's throw away was an almost vertical slope, falling one thousand meters down. It is true. It is in our Omani geology book. We could just see the source while lying on our stomach. It was difficult to get there, but the ladies managed to do it using a narrow path and a detour. There was no railing. We would not dare do it. In Marcel Pagnol's books about life in Province, France, a hundred years ago, you can read how important a source in the mountains is for a local community.

In olden days, people lived on a little shelf near the source. We saw remnants of old houses. Why were they abandoned? Because too many children fell down? Or did the times become more peaceful, so people did not have to live in such a dangerous, isolated place?

There were fossils all over. I returned home with a fossilized sea snail fifteen centimetres in diameter. Our geologists later said it was ninety-five million years old. Unfortunately, I did not find any fossilized dinosaur eggs. The landscape is fascinating, with a variety of colours caused by the fact that this part has mountains from various geological periods often in dramatic formations. When you came closer, you can see the causes of the different colours. At one site the rock was green due to copper. Another site was red due to iron, and at a third place was brown-black due to manganese, etc.

On the way home we stopped to have our five o'clock tea. We don't drink whiskey while driving, but later. We had a sandwich, and Allan told us the story behind the sandwich. The word sandwich comes from the Earl of Sandwich, who invented the sandwich while travelling by sea. While eating his invention, he could play cards at the same time. We enjoyed the combined soothing and stimulating effect of the tea while eating a cucumber sandwich, but without playing cards at the same time.

It occurred to me that it was now time to tell the true story about my colleague Dr Kumar of India. We both worked at The Royal Postgraduate

Medical School, London, from 1969–70 in professor Iain MacIntyre's laboratory, where we did experimental endocrinology. One day, Kumar was very angry because our boss, the professor, intended to go abroad for a meeting where he would talk about recent results from the laboratory, including some of Kumar's results. Kumar thought the results belonged to him, having not yet learned to appreciate the blessing of collaboration. He was angry, very angry, so angry that Sunday morning he drove to the professor's residence in order to kill him. He knocked at the door. The professor's wife opened it. There stood Kumar with a big knife in his right hand. "I want to kill your husband," said the angry man. "Please come in, Kumar. My husband will be back in a moment," Mabs said. They sat in the kitchen talking of the forthcoming murder. Iain's wife then said, "Let us have a nice cup of tea." When Iain came back, they sat quietly sipping tea.

That story proves the beneficial effects of tea on the human mind.

We talked of this unusual country, where women wear trousers and men long dresses, living like their forefathers had done for thousands of years. We pitied the people living in the mountains, who had to sell their homemade items to us, outsiders who drove into their world in our big cars, disturbing their peace. Perhaps they lead a better life than we do.

I would like to return to this pearl on earth, where there is plenty of space.

Preparations for Departure

I had twelve months leave from Denmark but had a two-year contract with the university here. Therefore, I had to break my Omani contract after a year, whereby the university saved my bonus, which corresponds to one month's salary. The people at the administration were nice to me. They wrote that they had been pleased to have me at the university. I liked them too. One gets used to their slow pace. They do not suffer from the rush of modern times. Westerners are too busy.

Now is August. They no longer die from heat exhaustion in India. But now they are drowned by their hundreds every day. The monsoon has come to India and Bangladesh.

After the unexpected rain at the anniversary of the Sultan's ascension to the throne, the desert near us has become somewhat greener.

Following a royal decree, the working hours have been changed. From 1 August, working hours will finish at four p.m., no longer at two thirty. The idea behind this change is the simple one that there should be identical working hours for privately and publicly employed persons. Until now, most Omanis have preferred public appointment because of the short working day. Now this might change. More work in the public sector is expected. No protests have been heard. People here do what they are told. There are no trade unions here. Those who don't want to work do not have to. They can stop, and let the family take over responsibilities.

We have recently celebrated the Prophet's birthday, the only birthday celebrated in Arab countries. We had a day off. We did not know the date. It was announced on the radio the day before. The date was decided by the Sultan after consultations with the Moon Sighting Committee. It was very conveniently a Wednesday so that everybody could have a long weekend. It is nice to have a day off in this heat. Likewise at home it is nice with a couple days off in the cold and dark period of 24 December and later. I am rather certain the Prophet did not know his birthday. I am also sure Jesus did not know his. Registration of birthdays did not begin in this country until 1970.

We shall soon again fly first class. There is nothing to do. You fly first class when flying down to Oman to work, and you fly back first class after you have worked in Oman for a period. You cannot swap the expensive return tickets to less expensive tickets to take you around the globe. I have tried. When departing, you arrive at the departure hall of the Seeb Airport, where you shall be met by an employee from the hospital administration. He'll give you your first-class ticket and your passport, which the administration has kept during you stay in Oman. They want to make sure you don't leave the country before the scheduled day.

I was a little silly arriving one year ago taking a night flight. You cannot eat a lot of Beluga caviar and drink a lot of champagne when you are tired. There are limitations.

Air transport to the Middle East and back is not always without problems. The biggest problem is overbooking. Some years ago I was invited to Oman to give lectures for a week. I was given a business-class ticket for Gulf Air starting in Frankfurt, where I arrived in due time. Naturally, I had reconfirmed my ticket seventy-two hours before, as required. Having arrived in Frankfurt Airport, I went in high spirits to the Gulf Air counter. My high spirits would not last.

"We are sorry; there is no room for you, but we can have seat for you some other day," I was told by a smiling, obliging lady. I had to puff myself up. I considered telling the smiling lady behind the counter that I was invited by the Sultan but rejected the idea. It was not true. His Majesty would most certainly have sent me a first-class ticket. Instead, I mentioned the Minister of Health, His Excellency Ali Bin Moosa. I said the Minister would not like to hear that I, his guest, could not arrive in time due to overbooking. I knew very well Gulf Air is owned by the governments of Bahrain, Qatar, the United Arab Emirates, and Oman. That helped. Before mentioning the minister I had heard the ladies mumbling about economy class. After my little remark about the minister, they suddenly had room for me on first class. Then again I had to start with Beluga caviar and champagne, excellent food, and vintage wines. I slept well.

It is now time to say good-bye to my colleagues. The other day I said good-bye several times. Having done that, and after having had a couple of drinks, I was a bit tipsy. The next day I met the man I had visited last. I felt I should apologize for my behaviour last night. He told me about his past in the British army. A young British officer was to receive the annual report on himself from his superior, his colonel. In it was this remark: "I regret to say I have seen this officer drunk." The young man was sorry to have this comment in print and asked the colonel to change that statement. "All right," the colonel said. "I'll delete the word drunk and write the word sober instead."

At the same occasion I learned how the drink gin and tonic, here termed G&T, was born. It was in India, then British India. Queen Victoria was empress of India. That title she had wanted in order to avoid that her daughter, married to the Crown Prince of Germany, should become empress before she did.

There were many cases of malaria among the British soldiers in India. Sometimes it was a problem, because the combat readiness was reduced due to disease. The doctors knew very well that quinine could prevent malaria and cure it. But it did not taste good, and the soldiers refused to take it. Then Indian tonic was invented containing quinine, and when you added some gin to it, the mixture was acceptable to the soldiers. It was even better when lime was added. That fruit came from Oman, and lime is still a successful Omani export article. And lime prevents scurvy (vitamin C deficiency).

Koran Reading

For some time I have been alone, without the family. I have been reading a lot. Most people have the Bible; I also have the Koran, a present from friends. Arabic to the right, English to the left. Comments in English at the bottom. One must remember to start from behind. It is easy to ascertain after a short time of Koran reading that Christians and Muslims are interrelated. Several legends are common, and in this country Jesus is recognized as a prophet of the same carat as Abraham and Moses, but he is not of the same quality as the Prophet Mohammed. Neither Jesus nor Mohammed wrote one single word in their lifetime, as far as we know. Perhaps they could not write. Perhaps they were illiterate. Only few were scribes.

A Westerner I know was talking with some Bedouins. He who speaks Arabic without an accent had no problems communicating with Arabs. They were sure he was a Muslim, since he was quoting the Holy Koran all the time. When they asked him directly he replied honestly that he was not. They then became very angry. They asked whether he believed in the Nazarene. Yes, he did. Friendship was transformed to hostility, until our colleague asked one of them to find a copy of the Holy Koran. He opened two different pages, showing them frequent mentions of Jesus. That helped, but they still thought believing in God, Jesus, and the Holy Spirit was the same as believing in many gods, and was something one should fight.

My Koran reading is still in its introductory phase. It has not yet convinced me that Islam recommends violence and intolerance, although one can read here and there that infidels should be killed, but that should perhaps not be taken literally. My impression is strengthened by listening to Koran recitations in English at seven a.m. on Muscat Radio.

The following could be read in the daily newspaper. Islam might never have seen daylight. It is told – and that is not in the Koran – that when Mohammed's mother was born, she was a problem for the family. She had an elderly sister and therefore could not be allowed to live. Her father took the newborn baby girl and buried her in the desert sand, as was the custom in those days. Having finished this rather unpleasant job, he saw the hand of the newborn come up through the sand. The child grasped the father's index finger. That was too much for him. She was allowed to live.

In ancient Scandinavia, they had similar habits. The unwanted child was left in nature, which then decided what should happen (starvation? cold exposure? eaten by wild animals?).

Oman allows the existence of Christian churches in contrast to Saudi Arabia. A number of my colleagues go to church regularly. Christian services are on Fridays. One has to know the scheduled services, because church bells are not allowed. The Omani citizens should of course be able to hear the call for prayer from the local mosque. It is possible to be buried from a Christian church. although the churchyard is hidden and can only be reached by sea. I have seen it myself.

Here tolerance prevails. In all Arab countries, it is important to answer correctly when you are asked about your religious persuasion. The right answer is that you are Christian. The wrong answer is that you are an atheist. Being an atheist is bad, very bad.

My respect for the Muslims of this country grows from day to day. Religion is part of daily life here, not only for the main festivals. Omanis do not lie, steal, or cheat. They do good deeds. They are kind, helpful, and forthcoming. They behave well, and treat Muslims and non-Muslims identically. They have nothing to do with the Muslim terrorists who exert their bloody trade in the name of Islam.

Resignation

The temperature is now forty-nine degrees, and there is almost 100 per cent humidity.

My resignation was accepted. I had to sign a paper proving I had received an acceptance letter. I shall now begin some hard work. I am going to try to be "cleared" (to be able to prove my bills have been paid, that I don't owe money to the bank, that I have returned my telephone, that I have not damaged my house, that I have not left any green plants in my "garden" [my terrace], that my borrowed software has been returned, that my ID sign has been destroyed, that my car has been sold, and that my sticker for the car [permission to drive through the university gate] has been removed).

I shall obtain quotations from three different forwarding agencies, from which the university will chose one. My goods will then be evaluated, and then we must see if there is overweight. At last I must not forget to book first-class tickets. Then I can get written proof that I have been here. This piece of paper must, however, be legalized by the Foreign Office of Oman, and that will take me a day or two. I begin to sweat thinking about it, but I am sweating anyway because of the high temperatures and the humidity.

Returning the telephone

One must expect to spend much time with formalities in Arab countries. For example, it will take some hours to discuss with the clerk Yacoob how to terminate one's close relationship with the telephone company. It is not simple. I hope it shall not be more difficult to getting rid of the telephone that acquiring it. That was difficult enough (see chapter 1). The most exciting part shall be trying to have the deposit back. Perhaps that will have to wait until next year? I must remember to mention that I have one of His Majesty's telephone lines.

It was worse than I had imagined. Off I went at eight o'clock in the morning in high spirits. The water for my morning shower was almost cool because the skies had been overcast. The air conditioning in my car could almost keep the temperature below the sweat limit. With a confident "good morning," I saluted my friends at the telephone company office, which was situated fifteen kilometres from home. I gave them my telephone apparatus. "Sorry, you have to return it on the other side of the motorway," one of them said kindly. Yacoob had informed me incorrectly. Yes, I could see the building.

I had to drive another fourteen kilometres to get there. Then I delivered the telephone once again. The nice man thanked me, asking if I had paid the last telephone bill. "No," I said. It had not yet arrived. Well, then he would make it ready. His computer reacted after five minutes. I was waiting. I noticed that the tariff had increased by 50 per cent. They had not informed us via newspapers as they usually do. I thanked the nice man and said I now would drive to the telephone ministry to receive my deposit after deduction of the last bill.

"No," the man said, smiling kindly, "the rules have been changed. First you have to pay, and then you can get your deposit back." Nobody had told me. Again back to the other side of the motorway with a receipt, a detour of another fourteen kilometres. I was now used to being sent to new excursions and expected that again. But no, I was permitted to apply for permission to return the telephone. Would I like to sit down? "But you already have the telephone," I protested.

He admitted that it was the case, and told me he thought the telephone was unnecessarily heavy for me to carry. Good argument. I filled in the application. He looked unsatisfied. It was written in Arabic, so I did not know what I had signed.

"There is no stamp," the nice man, Yousuf, said.

I thought by now I knew him so well I could use his first name. "But Yousuf, why do you not put a stamp down here in the lower right corner where there is room for it?" Sorry, he said, it should be the stamp of the university. When I had that, he would accept my application of returning the telephone.

Back to the university to my old friend, Yacoob. Twice fifteen kilometres. Yacoob had not left yet for prayer. He smiled obligingly. Was there anything he could do for me? I collapsed on a chair. He looked at me with sympathy. Finally I got my stamp.

Back to Yousuf. He also smiled kindly. Now he would accept my application of returning the telephone. He would now make my telephone bill for the last two weeks. "But I just paid the last bill," I said, exhausted.

He looked at me compassionately. That was only for July. It would take three days, perhaps a little longer, to register the calls for the last fourteen days, although they were already in the computer. There were so many bills, I was told. He looked overworked, showing me a list of five names. Perhaps he could only finish one customer per day. Yacoob had told me I could have everything right away ...

Worn down, I left. The telephone business was unfinished.

The tank had to be filled. The car runs 6.5 km/litre. This day's driving cost me almost a hundred Danish kroner (DKK), a huge sum. Petrol prices have gone up. They are now one-eighth of the prices in Scandinavia.

A New Friend

That evening I relaxed with Walther, the American military attaché, a new friend. Walther has many telephones. It gives me the shivers when I think of telephones. I must talk with my psychiatrist about it. Walther is a former fighter pilot and former professor of Middle East history, an interesting combination. He has lived for long periods in different Middle East countries. He is only forty-four and has not wasted his time. He speaks Farsi and Arabic fluently. I wondered what he was actually doing, asking if he was a spy.

"Of course," he replied laughingly. An interesting life. Other Americans were present. One of them was dealing in weapons. A very nice guy, who also spoke Arabic. He was probably also a spy. The head of Oman's electronic defence, Abdullah, was also present. Abdullah was naturally totally sober, since as a Muslim he does not drink alcoholic beverages. He refused to discuss the attempted coup against the Sultan. It was a bit embarrassing that I asked. Perhaps he is also a spy. I might be the only one present who is not. Abdullah taught me a great deal about electronic jamming. Later I was told he was one of the key figures in the tidying up after the attempted coup.

I asked Walther to tell his Pakistani cook and servant, Michael, that I liked the food he had prepared for us. He has been employed by the Americans for eighteen years, servicing the consecutive American military attachés. Perhaps Michael is also a spy? The only thing I can say with certainty is that I am not (yet) a spy.

We talked about the Gulf War and the situation in Iraq, but that I am not allowed to discuss with others. Incidentally, Walther was annoyed that Saddam had invaded Kuwait on his birthday, a couple of days after he had left, so he could not participate in the fun, sitting at home in Washington, watching the events on TV.

Finishing the telephone business

After an evening among Americans, I am now back in my Omani weekday. The administration has asked me to return all keys to the house. I was alarmed. "But then I cannot come in," I said. They had not thought of that, but they said I would probably find a solution to the problem. I did – I had extra keys made, but I did not tell them.

A week before our scheduled departure, I went to the city to collect my deposit of three hundred rials (about five thousand Danish kroner). I departed early knowing contacts with the telephone authorities take time. It is important be rested when you encounter those people in order to avoid becoming furious.

I entered my car trying to ignore that the outside temperature was forty-nine degrees and the humidity 90 per cent. My new telephone company friend, Yousuf, had given me the name of the man to contact to have the matter fixed. I went to the head office of the telephone company, reaching it after driving forty-five kilometres. I asked for Abdulla B. The man was not there. I must have looked angry, because his male Indian secretary looked frightened, saying his boss had "left for prayer." They usually say this when they are actually sitting somewhere behind a closed door having a power nap or reading the newspaper. If I could come back tomorrow? Then he would probably be present.

I felt my blood pressure rising dangerously while he was gesticulating. I told the young man I wanted the name and address of the permanent secretary. I intended to complain. I got the wanted information. With this I left, while the young person shouted, "The permanent secretary is at a meeting for the rest of the day and so is his deputy." My blood pressure rose to dangerous heights, while I was moving to the Ministry. That was only five kilometres away, a piece of cake. I had been there before.

It was a lucky day. It was one p.m., but a couple of the employees had not "gone to prayer." At the time I felt that the colour of my face might have been purple, as I was rather upset. The clerks at the cashiers' office treated me like a patient. They had nothing to do and found it interesting to play doctor. One of them called the office at the other side of the motorway and talked to Abdulla B., the man I had not been able to see, now having returned from "prayer." They then said it was very simple. I just had to go back and talk to Abdulla B. With a hysterical laugh I left the office.

Then again I entered the office where the Indian had shouted at me. He tried to hide under a table, but I spotted him. Abdulla B., who had returned from "prayer," was rested and fresh. He signed my papers. Now I should go back to the cashiers' office at the building on the other side of the motorway and talk to Khalid. Then everything would be fine. He smiled falsely. I knew the way.

Wet from sweat, I reached Khalid. I excused my sweating, saying, "It is hot today," to which he replied coolly, "It is hot every day." That was easy for him to say sitting there in his air conditioned office, while a multitude of clerks were chasing me from one building to the other. I had no time to avoid the midday sun, as Kipling had advised us all to do.

Khalid made the papers ready and said, "I'll now write the cheque." A sigh of relief from me. Then came an ominous addition: "Unfortunately, the permanent secretary and his deputy are at a meeting. Therefore, the signing of the cheque must wait until tomorrow." I offered to wait until four p.m. No, they will not be finished at four, and then the offices will close. I tried to explain to Khalid that I had driven far, and that Youssuf had told me it was a piece of cake to have my deposit returned. After all, it was my money.

He shook his head. "Normally it takes five days, but I'll make an exception, so the cheque will be ready tomorrow."

"But what if the gentlemen have a meeting tomorrow?" I asked.

He shook his head. It was obvious I was mentally deranged.

On the way home I stopped at a filling station. I had driven more than one hundred kilometres. I drank a couple of litres of water. Still I had not got my money. I forced myself to remember that I was paid for these strenuous hours, an exercise in self-control, which was not successful. It cost the hospital three working hours.

I got my cheque the next day.

After Summer

During my last days I am the administrative leader of the department. Not many students are left. During the waiting time until the next semester statistics are made, summer courses are arranged and makeup exams are finalized. Plans are made for the teaching during the next semester. The university teachers are studying to improve themselves.

There are enough problems to solve – problems with teaching and education, and problems with health in this country, where civilization as we know it has only been around twenty-five years. If this country is to not fall into poverty and social unrest when there is no more oil and gas, it is of paramount importance that the university is successful. His Majesty is right. Education is excessively important.

When the population is educated, perhaps people will begin to have fewer children.

In a short time, students and teachers will be back, and then comes a Swedish head of department. He can look forward to Oman.

Chapter 10

In which Oman is revisited

After 1994–95, my working year in Oman, the university invited me to come back eighteen months later to lecture on osteoporosis, a disease which is becoming increasingly common in Oman, perhaps due to the sedentary lifestyle of modern Omanis.

Everything was ready. Almost two hundred participants would come. I waited patiently, knowing visas often are received a couple of days before planned departure. Two days before my scheduled departure there was a fax for me. Visas for my wife and daughter. Nothing for me. I phoned, telling the people in charge that there was a mistake. No, there was no mistake. No visa for me. No explanation. I got the explanation the year after: having worked in Oman, you are not expected to come back in fewer than twenty-four months. Tourists can come as often as they wish. I was told it had something to do with competition. Not easy to understand.

Oman Seven Years Later

March 2001 was cold and windy. Snowstorm at Copenhagen Airport. An SAS flight to Frankfurt, followed by a Lufthansa flight from Frankfurt on time, arrival in Muscat at midnight as planned. The Germans are precise. The first thing noticed when leaving the plane was the warm air with the well-known scent of the tropics. A limousine from the Al Bustan Palace Hotel was waiting. Al Bustan Palace Hotel. A room with a sea view. It was nice to be

126

back. The Omanis are so nice, so polite, so calm, so friendly. Many are young. The Omani population is growing rapidly. We were here at the twenty-fifth anniversary of the "Renaissance," which took place starting in 1970, the time HM Sultan Qaboos took over. Now we are here at the thirty-first anniversary.

A lot has happened in the last six years. The Grand Mosque of Muscat is nearly finished, an architectural masterpiece. There are more flowers along the motorways than ever before, although there has been no rain for four years, but one has gas and oil for desalination of seawater. It is now Eid al-Adha. Our friend Mohammed from Baluchistan was not in his shop, but again in Mecca doing Hadj. We respect this religious man, whom we would have liked to meet again. The prices of his old silver jewellery have gone up several hundred per cent.

It might be common knowledge that the company Gulf Air is owned partly by the government of Oman. It was known for few delays and no accidents. It used to be run by British people, British pilots included. Due to omanisation, the British pilots were replaced by Omani pilots. The Omanis could fly themselves, they believed. But no. During a storm in Bahrain there was a problem: the Omani pilots could not land. By their third attempt the plane crash-landed in the water and all perished. We do not fly Gulf Air any longer.

At the hotel, omanisation goes rather well, but there are days the young servants stay at home (for example because a cousin is getting married, or a grandmother has died and there is going to be a funeral). Such family events are not uncommon. The families are big, and family members are close. Not long ago people here were Bedouins, and nobody told them what to do at a certain time. Time is not important here.

The students here often learn texts by heart, like when they studied the Holy Koran in school.

The students at the university are more fundamentalist than their parents. The aggressions against Israel are not insignificant, and the admiration for Saddam Hussein is not to be ignored. That creates problems. The professors were somewhat shaken recently when the students demonstrated in support of the new *intifada* (uprising) on the West Bank. Apart from that, the students are eager to learn, and they attend lectures as usual. For physiology, that is not good enough. You have to understand.

Haddia, my female colleague who speaks French, Arabic, and English in almost every sentence, quoted a female student who, after a physics course, came to her thanking her for a good course, adding: "Why do you have to mention God's name after each sentence?" Haddia laughed. She finishes each sentence by saying "voilà." The student heard it as "Allah."

Nick was kind and took us once more on a boat trip along the rocky coast of Oman. Already at eleven a.m. he said the famous words: "It is G&T time," and that day it was. He said, "I would rather have a full bottle in front of me than a pre-frontal lobotomy." But he also said that at sea it is important not to drink too much, for then you may not be able to do what you are supposed to do. Therefore, no *gisungusungu*. That means "dizzy" in Swahili. "Not to say drunk," says Nasser, our Omani friend who speaks Swahili fluently.

We knew very well that it is not without risk to swim in the waters of Oman. Some time ago Nick had invited a British visiting professor and his wife on a boat trip. The professor almost lost his wife that day. While snorkelling, she came close to dying from a severe allergic reaction to something in the water, perhaps a poisonous jellyfish. She survived thanks to the fact that the two gentlemen onboard were experienced physicians.

11 September 2001

I was at Hillerød Hospital, Denmark, when I heard that there had been an accident at the World Trade Centre, New York. An aircraft had, by accident we were told, crashed into one of the Twin Towers. I had been there some years earlier and had seen an aircraft flying below me. Like everybody else we were shaken when we heard the full story about the "accident" while watching everything on TV. In Oman, our friends also switched on the TV. Haddia too. Her younger son, a school friend of our daughter, had recently accepted an offer to come to work at the World Trade Centre after having graduated from Harvard. It was an ordinary working day. The work had begun in the offices. She was in shock, convinced her son was dead. She tried to call him. No reply. Then she was almost certain he was dead. Many hours later, when cell phone service was finally restored, her son called from New York telling his mother he was all right. His boss had asked him to come in at ten a.m., not eight.

Sometime later a big Anglo-American naval force sent cruise missiles on to Afghanistan and after that ground forces. The reactions of the Muslim Omani population? The clever Sultan can be trusted. There are two thousand British soldiers in the country and forty warships in Omani waters near Muscat. Probably they are now busy at Masira Island, where the RAF has a major air base. We all hope the Sultan will not fall ill or be assassinated. The allies should ask for his advice when a new Afghan government is to be established.

When we phoned our friends in Oman, we heard that everything was calm. Everybody praises the Sultan, who cleverly solves all problems in spite of fundamentalism.

Flying Back

We flew back with Lufthansa. We had two weeks with sun, temperatures around twenty-nine degrees, low-fat food, excellent service, and a lot of exercise. There was a stopover in Dubai, where we were waiting for a change of crew. A flight attendant asked over the loudspeaker if there was a doctor on the plane. Nobody reacted. I did so reluctantly. A German gentleman was not well. His wife said it was nothing. They'd had food poisoning the day before. She was all right, but he was not, was pale and sweating. He wanted to vomit but couldn't. I asked for a blood pressure device. Surprisingly they had one. His blood pressure was very low. I suspected coronary infarction. I asked if they had a medical clinic at the airport. They did. We went there, and I explained to the young Indian doctor there that I suspected coronary infarction.

Electrocardiography showed he had a big one, so he could not fly on. The captain asked what he could do for me, knowing the price for urgent landing in Kuwait. I said I would contact Lufthansa when I returned home. He did not ask me to move to business class, but Lufthansa later gave me a business-class ticket to Rio de Janeiro. Sudden cardiac death on a plane is no joke, and it is expensive.

We landed in frost, snow, and wind from the east.

Oman Twenty Years Later

It was time to go back to Oman. The weather in Northern Europe at this time of the year (February) is dark, windy, and cold, with occasional snow or rain, or even fog. The people look pale and depressed. A lot of them have vitamin D deficiency due to the lack of sun.

Oman in February is different. Agreeable temperatures, sun every day, a slight breeze from the Indian Ocean. Al Bustan Palace Hotel, the best hotel in the Middle East. Friendly and competent staff. Fantastic sea view from the room. Early morning coffee on the balcony, sun rising from behind the mountains in the East. The woman in my life had never been here before. We enjoyed every second. Sumptuous breakfast at the Al Khiran terrace. Swimming, snorkelling, being lazy in the sun. Getting a tan.

I had promised to show her the Muttrah soukh. We went twice. A man trying to sell us something was fascinated by her beauty and youth, noticing, I think, that she was considerably younger than me, and he asked curiously, "How long have you been married?"

"Many years," I said, which was not true. "And we have six children," which was true, although not with each other.

However, my reply impressed the man. Later that day, the Omani gentleman in the lobby offering us *kawa* (Omani coffee), which is well known for its scent of Omani rosewater, cardamom, and saffron, asked the same question, hinting that the lady was my second wife. He then whispered to her, "Try this frankincense every day, and he will not look for other women." He could not know that we did not have such a problem.

Muscat has gone through an extraordinarily rapid development since the Renaissance. Coming from a Europe with financial problems, stagnation, high taxes, high prices, and a general feeling of hopelessness, one finds it refreshing to be again in this country of optimism and increasing wealth. Although the Omanis complain that petrol has risen to 125 baizas per litre (equivalent to 0.875 Euros), people still buy 8-cylinder cars. The Sultan is said to consider abolishing subsidizing petrol prices. As said in one of the daily journals, there are no good reasons for families to have four big petrol-consuming cars, and no good reasons why this country should have petrol prices lower than the surrounding countries.

Income tax and VAT (value-added tax) have not (yet) been introduced. It is said that when written enquiries about the income of expatriates from tax authorities in Europe are received by Omani companies or government offices employing Europeans, no written answers will be sent. Personal income is a personal matter.

It is good for the financial situation of the country that large amounts of oil and gas plus copper and gold have recently been found.

His Majesty Sultan Qaboos bin Said is still immensely popular. He has guided his people through difficult times in recent years. Social and religious unrest, and even war, has been prevailing in neighbouring countries, but not in Oman. It is safer here than in Europe. Tourism is a rapidly developing industry in Oman, now that unrest in Libya, Algeria, Egypt, Lebanon, Syria, and Iraq keeps many Western tourists from going to those countries. Due to the farsightedness (good schools) of His Majesty, the young Omanis have an excellent command of English, making life easy for tourists in this country. His Majesty is not interested in tourists without money, only in tourists who can afford the hotels of Oman.

Chapter 11

Numbers and Statistics

I like the Omani newspapers in English. My favourite paper is *Times of Oman*, a well-edited, well-rounded newspaper with national and international news and excellent editorial comments. When in Oman, I read it every day. When not in Oman, I read it on the Internet. Here is some of what you could read in the Omani newspapers early 2014 and in recent official reports.

Unemployment

It is 18 February 2014 (18 Rabia II 1435 AH). The problem of unemployment is becoming serious: 15 per cent of Omanis are now without work. The explosion of the Omani population cannot match the creation of new jobs. The Manpower Ministry plans to reduce the number of expatriates working in the private sector from the current 39 per cent to 33.5 per cent. That would mean that around 100,000 jobs are to be stripped from expatriates and given to Omanis. More exactly, this would mean the number of expat workers would drop from 692,867 to 586,272, still a substantial number. How can this be done? Very simply by reducing the number of work permits or cutting down the duration of work permits. Many Europeans in Western Europe might dream that this would be possible in their country, where many jobs are taken over by people from

Eastern Europe. The national inhabitants in Europe must accept that they are replaced by foreigners. In Oman, jobs are given back to Omanis.

The Omani manpower minister is very well aware that Omanis cannot take over all jobs soon. Their skills have to be improved, and that is a major problem. Its solution will take time, so it is still possible for qualified foreigners to get good jobs in Oman.

Religion

One thing that strikes me whenever I am in Oman is the religious tolerance, the lack of the fanaticism which is so common in other Arab countries. During a week in February 2014, the British Minister for Faith and Communities, Sayeeda Warsi, visited Oman, the very first Muslim Minister of Great Britain, of Pakistani descent. She said, "The Sultanate of Oman is a perfect place where one can put aside any arguments between religious groups and pursue a path of mutual respect and understanding." She said something even more important: "Not only is religious freedom a good thing in itself, it is a good thing for economies and societies to progress." I think HM Sultan Qaboos agrees. Regarding Oman, she further said, "This country is an oasis of tolerance in a desert of divisiveness, proving that right in the geographical centre of a troubled region, different sects can live side by side." Speaking from the Grand Mosque, she added, "Today I hope I have made the case that violent sectarianism isn't just un-Islamic, it is anti-Islamic." Well spoken.

Christians and Muslims in Oman have always been able to practice their religion, unlike in Saudi Arabia and some other Islamic countries. The dominant branch of Islam in Oman is Ibadism, originating in the year 757. Ibadism is a moderate sort of Islam having hibernated in Oman, today the only survivor of the Khawarij, the oldest Islamic sect. Ibadism originated in Basra, now Iraq. It is usually regarded as an austere, puritanical, and tolerant religion, quite different from the Sunni and Shia sects. Ibadism is the foundation on which modern Oman is built. Ibadism is perhaps guiding His Majesty the Sultan and his government in their effort to modernize Oman. I have never been able to understand why Sunni and Shia Muslims can hate each other so intensely that they are able to kill each other. Ibadism is against confrontation. Ibadism is as new to many Westerners as it was to me. It is certainly not violent, and it might be the kind of moderate Islam so desperately wanted in the West, where Muslim extremism is difficult to comprehend. Let us try to understand what it is all about. Here are some key points:

1. Muslims will not see God on the Day of Judgment (shared with Shiites).
2. Whoever enters hell will remain there forever (Sunnis will only remain there for some time in order to purify their thoughts).
3. Ibadis do not impose the punishment of stoning for adultery. Nor do they use cutting off hands of thieves and beheading of criminals.
4. Ibadism favours that the emir is elected by the electorate, a democratic attitude.
5. It is not necessary for the ruler of Muslims to descend from the Prophet Mohammed.
6. It is unnecessary to have one leader for the entire Muslim world, and if no single leader is fit for the job, then Muslim communities can rule themselves (this is different from the Sunni belief of the Caliphate).
7. In Ibadism, conflicts are solved by debate, not confrontation.

Ibadism tries to follow Islam exactly the way the Prophet Mohamed thought and lived it. Ibadism returns to the purity of Islamic faith and society. In Ibadism one believes in a simple life. This might be the reason mosques in Oman are without much decoration. During the Friday prayer, blessing for tyrannical purposes is not permitted.

Climate

Oman has long and very hot summers. Rainfall is rare, mostly occurring during the winter months with an average of twenty to one hundred millimetres per year, mostly falling from December to April, often as a light drizzle. Rain in the Hajar Mountains can, however, be plentiful and cause flash floods during winter. The south-western monsoon occurs during summer in the Dhofar region in the south of the country.

The most popular time to visit Oman is between November and February, where day temperatures are pleasant, between twenty-five and thirty-five degrees Celsius, night temperatures ranging between seventeen and nineteen degrees. During summer, temperatures can exceed fifty degrees, and humidity can reach 100 per cent, a highly uncomfortable and somewhat dangerous combination which I have experienced a couple of times.

In the months June, July, and August, life is more agreeable in the Dhofar region than in the capital area and the Bathinah Coast, where many people live and work. The temperatures there are then usually ten degrees cooler. Due to rainfall during the monsoon period, the scenery is rather green with flowers all over. People from the north often travel south to enjoy the cooler climate there. The interior is often hot, with winds from the Rub' al-Khali desert, the air being drier there than the rest of the country.

Usually the winds are moderate, but there are occasional sand storms during winter. The dusty shamel winds occur in the capital area during summer, and often come in the morning, disappearing later during the day. Remnants of sand storms far away can be seen. Cyclones are rare, but two category five cyclones hit the country in 2007 and 2010.

Geography

One reason many tourists prefer Oman to other Arab countries is the variety and the beauty of the country. Oman has mountains, deserts, beaches, wadis, and lush greenery in the south. Oman has everything. The Wahiba Sands Desert has been described earlier in this book. Some other parts need description, it seems:

1. Musandam is an exclave forming the northern tip of Oman, being separated from the mainland of Oman by UAE (United Arab Emirates) territory. Here live 31,000 Omanis. The governate of Musandam covers 1,800 square kilometres. Musandam is known for its strikingly beautiful landscapes resembling the western part of Norway with deep fjords and mountains. The highest mountain is 2,087 meters. Musandam is of strategic importance due to its proximity to the Straits of Hormuz, through which passes 90 per cent of the oil from the Gulf States. The main city of Musandam is Khatab, a fishing village with a good port through which smuggling takes place, an illegal trade for the Iranians, a legal one for the Omanis. In comes cattle from Iran, out go TV sets, computers, etc. Musandam can be reached by air from Muscat, by boat from mainland Oman, and by car from the Emirates. Apart from Musandam there is another exclave, termed Madha, between Musandam and Muscat. It is rather small, only seventy-five square kilometres.

2. Jebel Akhdar is a dramatically beautiful mountain range in the Hajar mountains including Wadi Banni Auf, Jabal Shams etc. I have been there several times and enjoyed every second. The area is well known for its Mediterranean climate and fruits like peaches, pomegranates, apricots, plums, and figs, and for almonds, walnuts, and saffron, which is cheaper here than elsewhere in the world. The famous Omani rosewater is manufactured from roses grown here. Jabal Shams is the highest point in Oman, its peak being more than three thousand meters high. Unfortunately, it is not easy to visit the top. It is occupied by a military base, as it was twenty years ago when I was there.

Present Health Problems

The WHO (World Health Organization) and the World Bank consider that the health system of Oman performs well, providing universal access for Omanis without excessive spending. Life expectancy for Omanis living in Oman continues to rise. Statistics have improved. The following figures are available from public sources.

The development of life expectancy has been as follows (mean of men and women): 1960: 41.9 years; 1970: 50.1 years; 1980: 60.6 years; 1990: 69.9 years; 2000: 73.7 years; 2011: 72.3 years, the latest decline remaining unexplained, but perhaps the rise in life expectancy is levelling off. The well-known difference between men and women has always been seen in Oman. The women have always lived longer than the men. In the year 2011, the average of 72.3 years hides a marked difference between men and women. That year the life expectancy for men was 70.4 years, for women 75.6 years.

The extraordinary increase in life expectancy does not come from nothing but from specific investments. During the period from 1970 to 2010 the number of hospitals, private clinics, doctors, nurses, pharmacists and other health workers increased significantly.

	Doctors	Nurses	Dentists
1970	13	?	0
1980	514	1,096	23
1990	1,441	4,147	84
2000	3,258	7,829	262
2010	5,862	12,.865	654

The Department of Family and Community Medicine at the Sultan Qaboos University Hospital was performing well when I worked at the hospital twenty years ago. The Department of Family Medicine was established in 1987 to teach undergraduates. It is a well-known fact that countries with good primary care have lower overall health costs than less fortunate countries. Until 2009 a total of 110 Omani doctors had graduated as family physicians. It is planned that in the next five years there shall be a family physician for each of the 159 health centres in the country.

There has been an interesting development of the private health sector in recent years. From 2003 to 2012, the number of private hospitals increased from three to eleven, while the number of government hospitals remained constant at fifty-four. Why is the private hospital sector becoming so popular? Because the waiting time is short, and because the private hospitals have been able to recruit skilled foreign specialist doctors.

The most frequent causes of death in Oman are 1. coronary heart disease; 2. high blood pressure; 3. diabetes; 4. stroke; and 5. kidney disease. The three first ones are typical lifestyle diseases. One of the biggest problems of later years is the increasing incidence of type-2 diabetes, even among children.

The prevalence of diabetes in the Gulf countries is the highest in the world. A total of 12–15 per cent of the Omani population have diagnosed diabetes, but undoubtedly the total number is much higher, because this disease can remain silent and undetected for a long time.

Cardiovascular diseases in Oman are also frequent, like diabetes being attributed to the sedentary lifestyle here. Many have the unfortunate combination of high blood pressure and diabetes. It is believed that consanguinity is a major problem here, with 34 per cent of Omanis being married to a first cousin. This cultural phenomenon might be responsible for a major part of the increasing incidence both coronary heart disease and diabetes. According to official reports, 42 per cent of the deaths in Oman can be attributed to cardiovascular disease, which is often seen in conjunction with diabetes. However, in contrast to the Western world, cancer is rather rare here, causing only 12 per cent of the deaths in Oman.

Regarding cancers, their distribution also differs from countries of the West. Thus the five most frequent cancers in Oman are 1. leukaemia; 2. non-Hodgkin's lymphoma; 3. prostate cancer; 4. stomach cancer; and 5. lung cancer. Currently, more and more Omanis smoke, but smokers are less abundant here than in the West, 13 per cent of Omani men being smokers and 0.5 per cent of the women.

Infectious diseases are of course a problem in Oman, but not like in Africa. Malaria is almost eradicated except in Musandam and in certain wadi pools. Trachoma is rapidly declining. Sand flies are carriers of leismaniasis, which leads to skin lesions and open sores. Middle East respiratory syndrome coronavirus (MERS-CoV) is present here like in other parts of the Middle East, but quantitatively this virus is a minor problem. A total of 414 people (2014) have died in the Middle East since this virus first emerged. It is believed this virus is transmitted by camels. AIDS is of course a problem also in Oman, where extramarital affairs are seen but not talked about.

In 2004 a total of 15 per cent of girls married between fifteen and twenty years of age, resulting in a rather young and uneducated population of young mothers. In theory, both male and females have the right to choose their spouse, but it is still common that the father finds the husband for his daughter.

During the period between 2003 and 2012, fertility increased considerably, with 24.4 births per 1,000 people in 2003 rising to 32.1 births per 1,000 people in 2012. This is, of course, worrying, showing that the recent history of birth control in Oman is not a success story, perhaps not surprising for a country where you can meet men with thirty children and four wives.

Infant and maternal mortality are now low, maternal mortality being as low as in the United States. Congenital anomalies account for 28 per cent of the early neonatal deaths. The Minister of Health stated April 2014 that when infant mortality is expressed as deaths before the first year has elapsed, the numbers are the following: 1970: 118 deaths per 1000 children; 1985: 45 deaths per 1000 children; 2012: 9.5 deaths per 1000 children.

Medical research is not thriving in Oman, but Oman now has two peer-reviewed internationally recognized medical journals: *Sultan Qaboos University Medical Journal*, and *Oman Medical Journal*. Medical research is beginning to surface.

Law and Order

Oman is a country where many people want to live and work. Not everybody has the right papers, perhaps not a work permit, perhaps not a sponsor. A sponsor is mandatory if you want to work here. Of course you can enter as a tourist and then "disappear," but few do that due to travelling costs. You can also try to cross the border illegally and see what happens. Every day foreigners are arrested at the borders having tried to enter the country illegally. They are turned back to where they came from. Some are jailed. Unlike in Europe, they are not kept in camps for months and years until a judge decides whether they may stay or not. Some Europeans might envy Oman having such a system.

The Omani police are apparently good. The crime rate in Oman is low. One feels safe here, safer than in Europe and America. Thefts and burglaries are extremely rare. So are violent crimes. Homicide frequency decreased from 1995 to 2000, from 0.94 to 0.91 per 100,000 population.

Drug trafficking is, however, growing like in other countries, but compared to the West it is a minor problem. There are reports of women being victims of trafficking, and it does happen that foreign young women working as house maids do so under slave-like conditions.

The attitude towards beggars is also different here. In Muscat there is an anti-begging squad. They held more than five hundred beggars in 2013, some of them children. Many were turned over to the Omani police. Begging is not allowed. The system seems to work. I have never seen a beggar here.

Some problems of law and order seem quite trivial. As noted earlier, twenty years ago we could not get through the university gate if our car was dirty after a desert trip. Car wash first, then enter. Similarly, now you can be fined in Muscat, if the police see that your car is dusty or dirty. Another problem of insignificance: it has been decided that the shopkeepers at the Muttrah soukh may no longer exhibit their goods in front of their shops as has been the custom for centuries. No, the shopkeepers must keep them inside, a rule that after a few weeks meant a significant drop in sales. If they do not obey, their shops will be closed after three days.

Recently there were demonstrations against corruption in the country. The Sultan listened to the voice of his people. A former managing director of a company was found guilty of bribery five times. He gave bribes to PDO employees to facilitate the awarding of contracts to his firm. Sentence:

three years in jail for each offence, a total of fifteen years in jail. Also, he had to pay 1,774 million Omani rials in fines. He will not do it again. Another case is worse for the culprit. The Court of First Instance in Muscat sentenced the CEO of state-owned Oman Oil Company to twenty-three years in jail for accepting bribes, abuse of office, and money laundering. There is certainly law and order here.

Transition to Democracy

Some foreigners believe the transition to democracy may be rapid. The Sultan knows better. Democratization must proceed slowly if it is going to work. In 1997, the Sultan decreed that women could vote and stand for election to the Majlis al-Shura, the consultative assembly of Oman. Today many members are women. All citizens above the age of twenty-one may vote. It is difficult to assess the influence of this consultative body, but so far the Sultan governs by decrees.

Democracy is coming slowly to the Sultanate of Oman. His Majesty knows that in politics you should not have exaggerated confidence in amateurs.

We live in a changing world. Nowadays Oman is more and more oriented towards the Far East. Fifty per cent of international passengers travel to South-East Asia by air. Trade relations between Oman and that part of the world are being cultivated. Whether that facilitates democratization is another matter.

Progress is not necessarily accompanied by loss of cultural identity. The Sultanate of Oman is exceptional in many ways, one aspect being that it has kept its traditions in spite of modernization.

Traffic

There are no railways or waterways in Oman. Bus driving is not popular, being regarded as a sign of poverty. The Omanis prefer travelling in their own private car, which makes sense, since cars and petrol prices are low and the Omani roads excellent, most of them being dual carriageways, lit up at night, and well equipped with traffic signs and traffic lights.

However, there are problems with the Omani drivers.

The number of Omani cars has been increasing in recent years. During the years 2000–09, it increased more than the growth in population. Similarly, motorization increased during that period by 26 per cent, mostly due to privately owned cars. In the year 2009, there were 230 cars per 1000 population, a rather high number.

There were 2.67 accidents per 1,000 population. Seventy per cent of road accidents happened to drivers seventeen to thirty-six years of age, mainly due to speeding. Drunk driving is rare, since drinking alcohol is against the Holy Koran. Speed limits exist and are well signposted, but one has the impression the young drivers consider them as guidelines only. Road traffic accidents is the number one cause of accidental injuries in Oman, most of the cases being collisions, often frontal collisions. A total of 10 per cent of road accidents were fatal in the year 2009 with 760 deaths. The number of road accidents has been declining during the period 2000–09 from 13,040 to 7,252, a drop of 44 per cent, perhaps due to increasing awareness of the dangers of speeding or perhaps due to the increasing risk of being spotted by the police.

The Minister of Transport and Communication recently disclosed that the government has plans to develop a ferry transport system along the coastal stretches of the capital area in order to diminish the rapidly increasing traffic on the already congested roads.

Another government project is considerably more comprehensive, and is, in fact, a mega project. It is about railways. There are plans to build a railways network in order to tie the different regions together; connect Oman with the neighbouring countries; and enable the big ports (such as that of Salalah) to become main gates for export/import for the Gulf countries. This plan is not for beginners. Here we are talking about a railway system of 2,244 kilometres. Diesel, not electricity, will be used to operate the railways. Perhaps the minister should ask in Europe how their experience with Diesel locomotives might be.

Education

The Sultan thinks of the future, a future without oil and gas, a future which is not far away. In that not-too-distant future, it will be important to have an educated population. The school system here has improved in recent years. A result of this is that the literacy rate for people older than fifteen has increased from 55 per cent in 1990 to 81 per cent in 2006, and for those fifteen to twenty-four from 86 per cent to 97 per cent, a rather remarkable achievement which cannot be matched by many countries.

Oman's official educational program is rapidly expanding. The basic education covers the first ten years of schooling. This is followed by two years of post-basic schooling where you can study the classic subjects: Latin, Greek, Hebrew, Arabic, and ancient Sanskrit, if you are interested. The Sultan Qaboos University, where I used to work and teach, offers higher education in medicine, arts, social sciences, commerce, education, law, nursing, agriculture, and marine science. Like twenty years ago, one year or two years of English is presently mandatory before you are allowed in. The university is an English-speaking school, situated in the Middle East, with English textbooks. Why English? Because they are the best, His Majesty believes, and His Majesty is right.

A new educational reform is now being implemented. One feature of the reform is about developing human resources in times of decreasing reliance of oil and gas income. Another feature is that the education in the coming years will be synonymous with the advancement of the female population. Women are expected to contribute significantly in all sectors of Omani life in the years to come.

History

The Portuguese were here first. They came to Oman in 1497. The Portuguese occupied the coastal regions of Oman for 143 years. During that period the flourishing trade with China declined. No European power ever conquered the entire country. Oman was a large country from the seventeenth century with control extended to areas that are now Iran and Pakistan. Zanzibar was part of Oman, and the Sultan often ruled his large country from there.

In the nineteenth century, Oman came under the influence of the British, whose navy needed a stop on their way to British India. However, Oman was never a British protectorate or colony. The British treated the Omanis well, and the British influence is still extraordinary here.

In 1747, the al Said dynasty came to power after having ousted Persian occupying forces, and even today the fourteenth Sultan of this dynasty, Sultan Qaboos, rules the country.

The Dhofar region was regarded by the old Sultan, Sultan Qaboos's father, as his private property rather than part of Oman. In 1962, a dissatisfied tribal leader founded the Dhofar Liberation Front, obtaining arms from Saudi Arabia. The Saudis had already supported two insurrections in the Jebel Akhdar from 1957 to 1959.

During the final stage of the rebellion 1959 the rebels fled to the Jebel Akhdar where they found a mountain peak which they believed was defendable, but they did not know the SAS (special air services) a famous British regiment, renowned for unusual solutions to difficult military problems. Two squadrons of the regiment scaled the southern face of the mountain, which was so steep it was considered impossible to climb. The rebels were sure they could sleep in peace, which they did, but SAS could climb, and the rebels were taken by surprise in their sleep. Then supplies were parachuted to the British soldiers. Those of the rebels who were not killed fled to Saudi Arabia.

As described elsewhere in this book, Sultan Qaboos took over in a palace coup in 1970 and became the fourteenth Sultan of the Busaidi Dynasty. The day was 23 July 1970, the day that later became the Renaissance day. His father, Sultan Said bin Taimur, was deported that very day.

The first problem the new Sultan faced in 1970 was the continuous armed communist insurgency originating in neighbouring South Yemen. The rebellion was named after the southern province of Oman, the so-called Dhofar rebellion. That problem was dealt with by the young Sultan Qaboos. Aid was coming in from the Shah of Iran, King Hussein of Jordan, the SAS, and the British Royal Air Force. From those days until today, Britain remains a close friend and ally of Oman. The British forces were not supposed to be there when it all began. The British prime minister, Edward Heath, did not want the press to deal with the Omani adventure. It started in 1970 when 25 troops from the SAS arrived. The SAS distinguished themselves at the battle of Mirbat in 1972, where a small SAS force with Omani support beat a far bigger enemy force of 250 guerrillas. Not many in the West knew about this, because it was a secret war. Western powers were not officially involved, although it was known that Britain had sent "advisors." Why was that battle so important? Because it prevented the communist guerrillas reaching the Straits of Hormuz. That would have had the potential of changing the power balance in the world. From then the Sultan had the upper hand, with continuous help from Britain.

Foreign Policy

It appears there are some main principles governing the foreign policy of Oman:

- adapting to changing circumstances
- remaining non-aligned
- avoiding intervention and confrontation
- seeking compromise
- never harbouring hostile intentions

The Sultan was one of the founders of the GCC (Gulf Cooperative Council), where he has great influence. Oman pursues a moderate foreign policy and has expanded its diplomatic relations dramatically. Oman has friendly ties with all neighbouring countries after having settled all border disputes, even with Yemen, a former adversary. When Iraq invaded Kuwait, Oman participated in the UN liberation efforts and gave the United States access to facilities in Oman, without interrupting the diplomatic ties with Iraq.

His Majesty a long time ago invited the prime minister of Israel, Mr Rabin, to visit Oman, which he did. Oman did not break the diplomatic ties with Egypt after President Sadat signed the treaty with Israel recognizing Israel. Other Arab countries did. In 1994 he invited the Israeli government to attend a conference on water desalination, an important subject in the Arab world.

While other nations in the Middle East have been driven by ideology and hatred, the Sultanate of Oman has pursued its own course of peaceful negotiation, which is so essential for safety and prosperity. The Sultan is an advocate of gentle diplomacy.

He is maintaining friendly ties with Iran. The Iranian president, Mr Rouhani, visited Oman in March 2014. Newspapers were unexpectedly open-minded, stating that the visit aimed at boosting bilateral relations between Iran and Oman, and also might ease tensions between Iran and the West. A deal was signed for a 350 kilometre underwater gas pipe line from Iran to Oman for transportation of gas to Oman and further on from Omani ports. It would appear that such a gas pipeline would lessen the strategic importance of the Straits of Hormuz, the common Omani and Iranian waterway.

His Majesty has always been an excellent mediator. According to people here the Sultanate was site of some of the recent secret talks between Iran and the United States, resulting in the landmark nuclear deal in November 2013. Interestingly, the Sultan was the first foreign leader to visit President Rouhani in Teheran after he took office.

Finances

Oil was first discovered in 1964, and oil production began in 1967. Everything is coordinated by PDO. The government owns 60 per cent and Shell 34 per cent of PDO. According to official Omani sources, Oman relies on oil and gas for 87 per cent of its budget revenue. Although oil production is of paramount importance for the country, there has been a decline in the net oil revenue which unfortunately goes along with increased government spending, a rise of 10.1 per cent from January 2013 to January 2014. According to financial advisors this might lead to increased borrowing and selling of foreign assets. In spite of these problems, which might be temporary, the average per capita income has increased significantly over the years, going from $4,674 US in 1980 to $23,351 US in 2010, an impressive achievement.

PDO has announced that it shall donate a giant aquarium of seventeen thousand square meters marking the forty-fifth anniversary of the Renaissance next year (2015), a gift to the nation worth 7.5 million Omani rials.

Oman has a goal, it seems, that progress shall not necessarily be accompanied by loss of cultural identity. The oil adventure has certainly not destroyed the cultural identity of Oman. On the contrary, it has made it possible to cultivate some aspects of Omani culture.

Epilogue

This is the end of my stories from Oman, a tale of a modern Arab country, which in fewer than fifty years has achieved what Europe needed five hundred years to accomplish. May others come to love this country, which in its modern form is the result of a unique cooperation between a clever ruler and a most civilized country, Great Britain.